FIRE IN THE CHURCH

FIRE IN THE CHURCH

By

Ted. S. Rendall

Foreword by

Theodore H. Epp

moody press
chicago

This book is dedicated to the Spirit of
the living God, to whose presence and
power the seasons of refreshing that the
church has known in this dispensation
are to be traced. It is our prayer that He
may employ these studies both to create
a desire in the hearts of His people for
revival and to guide them in their
experience of revival.

© 1974 by

THE MOODY BIBLE INSTITUTE
OF CHICAGO

ISBN: 0-8024-2635-2

Printed in the United States of America

CONTENTS

SEND A GREAT REVIVAL, LORD!

In my heart, dear Lord, I pray,
 Send a great revival;
Take me, use me day by day,
 Send a great revival.

Power for service, Lord, I crave,
 Send a great revival;
Help me some lost soul to save,
 Send a great revival.

Give me grace Thy will to do,
 Send a great revival;
As I now my vow renew,
 Send a great revival.

Thine alone, Lord, I would be,
 Send a great revival;
Let it now begin in me,
 Send a great revival.

Send a great revival, Lord,
Send a great revival, Lord,
Send a great revival, Lord,
 And let it NOW begin in me.

AUTHOR UNKNOWN

6

FOREWORD

I AM PLEASED to recommend this book by Ted S. Rendall on revival. Sometimes those speaking and writing about revival give an emphasis that is not found in the Scriptures, but Mr. Rendall is not guilty of this. The author does an excellent job of bringing all matters of consideration into the light of what God's Word says rather than using an argument from experience.

Concerning the lack of revival today, Mr. Rendall narrows it down to the crucial reason when he says, "Let's face the fact in honesty and humiliation—the reason for the shut heaven is the sin of God's people." Obedience to the Word of God is emphasized throughout this volume as being necessary if we are to have revival today.

Although Mr. Rendall points out some of the common characteristics of past revivals, he stresses that we are not to be geared to the past but are to be concerned primarily with what God is able to do today.

Not only is Ted Rendall knowledgeable of revivals of the past, but also he has been in the midst of revival on the Prairie Bible Institute campus. After a revival had taken place on the campus in 1972, there was highly significant counsel given in the June 1972 *Prairie Overcomer* (official organ of PBI). Taking a rightful stand against experience-based Christianity that is so prevalent today, this counsel was the following:

> The preaching of God's Word should not be wholly set aside in times of spiritual awakening. There are great themes relevant to the needs of those whose hearts are being revived that should be preached during such times of revival. Hungry

7

hearts cannot be fed and strengthened on a diet of testimonies, no matter how striking they may be.

The attitude of some has been substantially this: "Oh, well, we've had preaching for years, and what did it ever do for us? What we need now," they say, "is not more preaching, but more opportunity for sharing." We reply, "The preaching of godly pastors in past years may not have brought the revival that we are now seeing. But surely their preaching laid a foundation for the Spirit's working."

May this book be used of God in bringing revival to your own soul.

THEODORE H. EPP

PREFACE

IN HIS WELL-WRITTEN BIOGRAPHY of Gypsy Smith, David *ill. on* Lazell retells a story often told by the English evangelist. *Revival* On one occasion Samuel Chadwick, then principal of Cliff College, Methodism's "School of the Prophets," received a telephone call from someone seeking a preacher for a service on the following Sunday.

Thinking over those who would be available, Mr. Chadwick responded, "Well, you can have Mr. Jones, but, if you have him, you'll have a revival."

"Oh, dear," said the startled caller. "We don't want that!" And the line went dead.[1]

This book is unashamedly about revival, and, lest you be tempted right now to turn off its message, here are some reasons you should continue to read (and hopefully to ask God for His deeper work in your life and in your church).

First, without doubt, there is a religious awakening in North America. But that very fact demands that evangelical Christians restudy the biblical principles of revival. "Does all the noise we hear herald a genuine religious revival? Will the new kinds of interest fade away, or will they endure? What effect will they have on traditional religion as we have known it? What is the outlook for religion?" These are questions raised by the editors of *The Religious Reawakening in America*,[2] and we can only begin to answer those questions when we understand something of the theology of revival as taught by the Scriptures.

Second, it is our conviction that genuine spiritual revival has been experienced in various parts of North America in recent years.[3]

9

Some writers on the subject of revival have insisted that revival is purely an individual matter and that we should not expect revival that will touch and change a church or a community. But it is not necessary to introduce such an emphasis. Revival is both personal in its demands and social in its outworking. We can see spiritual awakening that changes lives, homes, churches, and communities.

Third, although written some years ago, the following words of John Thomas of Wales, clearly summarize the tension facing some Christians today, especially those who hold to a pretribulational and premillennial viewpoint of our Lord's second coming:

> We are being caught at present between two currents in the evangelical world. With a great number of earnest Christians the emphasis of the hour is laid on the expectation of our Lord's return to close the present age, and this emphasis is so pronounced that the expectation of a great religious revival is almost ruled out. The longing for, and expectation of, our Lord's glorious return has in a measure substituted itself for the old passionate longing for the descent of the spiritually quickening power of Pentecost.
>
> But it is equally true that, although with less self-assertion and demonstration, there is a great longing in the hearts of thousands of believers for the advent of another great day of spiritual revival rather than for the abrupt closing of the present age. My belief is that this desire is growing in intensity and in assurance, and that a great many whose expectation has been focused on the glory of the skies, are finding it possible to return to an earnest expectation of the spiritual glory of the "upper room." Two such mighty expectations should not be allowed to cancel each other, but to work together for one glorious end.[4]

These, then, are some of the reasons why you should read about revival. It is my prayer that, whether these studies are used by individuals or by groups, the response will be, "Revival? We want that!"

ACKNOWLEDGMENTS

My thanks to Dr. Theodore Epp for his gracious foreword and to my wife, Norline, for her patient typing of the manuscript.

REVIVE US AGAIN!

Lord, Thou hast with favour
  Smiled upon our land,
Yet the powers of darkness
  Press on every hand;
And the hearts that love Thee
  Often cry in pain—
Wilt Thou not revive us,
  Revive us again?

Precious, guileless children
  To our homes are given,
That our love might win them
  To the life of Heaven;
Yet what snares and pitfalls
  Make our labour vain!
Oh, to save the children,
  Revive us again!

Deep in heathen darkness
  Blood-bought millions wait
For a voice to tell them
  Of their ransomed state;
Break the spell that binds us
  But to selfish gain!
By Thine own compassion,
  Revive us again!

Wilt Thou not revive us,
  Revive us again?
For our nation's sake
And for Jesus' sake,
  Revive us again!

W. LESLIE

1

THE PATTERN OF REVIVAL

I will remember the years of the right hand of the most High.—PSALM 77:10

"YEARS OF THE RIGHT HAND of the most High." No words could more adequately define the seasons of revival that have periodically blessed the Christian church throughout her history. Such revivals are best described as years in which the power of God has been dramatically experienced by men and women.

Yet, strange and sad to say, many Christians today are unfamiliar with these momentous movements of God the Holy Spirit among His people. Further—and this is the primary reason for our consideration of the pattern of revival—many believers are totally unconcerned about the subject of revival and are not praying definitely for "times of refreshing from the presence of the Lord" (Ac 3:19).

We do well, therefore, to heed and follow the example of the psalmist and deliberately to "remember the years of the right hand of the most High." Such a review of God's activity among His people will quicken our languishing hearts, revive our fainting spirits, and rekindle the prayer of faith.

WHAT PRECEDES SEASONS OF REVIVALS?

In thinking, then, of the pattern of revival, let us inquire first with regard to *what precedes* such "years of the right

13

hand of the most High." That is, we are to consider *the reason for revival.*

Isaiah predicted a time when "darkness shall cover the earth, and gross darkness the people" (Is 60:2). Without doubt, this general condition of moral and spiritual darkness precedes seasons of revival. And when revival does come, the word of the Lord is, "Arise, shine; for thy light is come, and the glory of the Lord is risen upon thee" (Is 60:1). Then the day breaks, and the shadows flee away (Song 2:17).

This intense darkness covers both the world and the church.

Historians of revivals of the past have carefully shown in their writings that "gross darkness" covered and cloaked the world of unregenerate men immediately prior to times of quickening in the church.

Thus, writing on "Prevailing Conditions" in the United States just before the revival of 1857, Ernest M. Wadsworth stated:

> The conditions in [18]57 were like those facing the Church today. The country was much smaller than now, but the sins and the untoward conditions were about the same. At the time approaching that divine visitation, Americans were living in idle luxury. Wines were plentiful. The theatre and the dance had gripped a pleasure-bent people. Divorce was easy in the new states. Feminine smokers were numerous. Free love, gambling, robbery, murder, and mob-administration were widespread, not only in the "wild and woolly West," but everywhere. Sunday was a day of pleasure. Vicious cults like Spiritism and Mormonism captured the minds of thousands.
>
> The nation was generally prosperous. . . . Buying, selling, and money-making occupied the minds of businessmen to the exclusion of better things. Newspapers increased. Secular reading was sold cheaply. Large numbers of papers and books were bought by eager readers. . . . Infidelity and atheism were rampant. . . . Prosperity gave the people much leisure time for reading and discussion. . . . The consciences of men became hardened. Indifference to spiritual religion generally prevailed.[1]

We could add many quotations to illustrate the fact that before "years of the right hand of the most High," the tide of moral and spiritual life has been at the lowest ebb. And need we point out how the conditions in 1857, as described by Mr. Wadsworth, strikingly approximate those of our space age?

Turning now to consider the Christian church, we discover that here, too, just prior to times of general awakening, there have existed conditions of moral and spiritual darkness. In his discussion of revivals of the past, the Rev. John Shearer wrote of the situation in England during the early part of the eighteenth century:

> The eighteenth century opened for England in deep spiritual gloom. The Puritan fire was almost extinct, and a cold Deism that hardly troubled to guise itself, reigned in the Church. A gross darkness covered the people. The court was foul. Vice walked naked and unashamed. In the high circles of government, bribery had become a fine art.[2]

Conditions in the church, therefore, prior to periods of revival may be summed up thus: widespread apostasy and the increase of false doctrine throughout Christendom along with lukewarmness and listlessness in orthodox and fundamental circles.

R. B. Jones has stated quite clearly the moral and spiritual conditions that precede "years of the right hand of the most High" when he wrote,

> Each revival comes in a time characterized by confusion, politically and morally; by the spread of sacerdotalism; by social lawlessness and chaotic homelife; by worldliness in the churches and skepticism in the pulpits.[3]

J. Edwin Orr once had a conversation with Evan Roberts, who was so mightly used in the Welsh revival of 1904-05.

"People ask me, my brother," said Roberts to Orr, "if I see any signs of the revival for whose coming we all pray. Now, as you travel about, you may see the positive signs, but I am not so privileged just now. I tell them that I see all the negative signs. The churches seem to be at rock-bottom in their decline. The turning point is at hand.

"Indeed," he went on, "I would compare the state of the true Church today with the state of the prodigal son in the far country *just before he went home to his father*. Mark you, he has not started for home yet. . . . He is still among the swine and the husks, but he is 'utterly fed-up.' As I would have said of the prodigal son, 'He won't be there much longer'—so I predict of the Church as it is today."[4]

Evan Roberts' statement was made before World War II. What would he say if he were alive today?

To those who claim, therefore, that conditions are beyond the possibility of revival, a careful and candid investigation of the past will serve to show that revival has always been preceded by times of darkness and declension and depravity. D. M. Panton wrote, "It is a foolish blunder to suppose that any age can be too evil for revival."[5]

WHAT PRECIPITATES BLESSING OF REVIVAL?

Having looked at the conditions that precede "years of the right hand of the most High," we are better prepared to understand *what precipitates* the "showers of blessing" that are experienced in periods of revival. That is, we are now seeking to understand *the road to revival*. God has pledged His Word to His people. "I will pour water upon him that is thirsty, and floods upon the dry ground" (Is 44:3). He has promised "showers of blessing" (Eze 34:26) and "times of refreshing from the presence of the Lord" (Ac 3:19). What, then, precipitates these showers upon the dry ground?

Before dealing in detail with those factors in the Christian church which, by God's Spirit, have contributed to revival, we should notice that in some cases, revival has been preceded by a crisis in the economy of the nation where the awakening has later taken place. Frank G. Beardsley pointed out that although the revival of 1857 was "preceded by a time of financial and commercial prosperity unprecedented in the history of the United States," the year 1857 brought a sudden reversal, and the nation was thrown into a financial panic.[6]

It is within the Christian church, however, that revival commences. It is this aspect of spiritual renewal concerning which Leonard Ravenhill's words hold true: "There is no pattern for revival. Though babes are everywhere born by the same process, how different the babes themselves are—all new, no repeats! By the very same process of soul-grief and protracted prayer and burden because of barrenness, revivals of all ages have come—yet how different the revivals themselves have been!"[7]

And yet, while we cannot schedule the birth of a revival, we can learn from the past; we can consider what has precipitated showers of blessings in other countries and in other centuries.

First, there has arisen within the church a group (or groups) of God-fearing men and women who have become concerned about the need for revival. This holy remnant has always been deeply conscious of the reproach cast upon the name of the Lord by the low spiritual state of the church. It has also been acutely aware of God's displeasure with His people in their lukewarm condition (Rev 3:15-16). This heart concern for revival has found expression in a heart cry for revival. Prayer—agonizing prayer—has been offered that God might revive His church, declare His glory, and make bare His mighty arm of salvation.

It is to be noted that often this nucleus of praying men and women has been composed of obscure members of the church. Thus, Charles G. Finney wrote,

17

Go and inquire among the obscure members of the church and you will always find that somebody has been praying for a revival, and was expecting it—some man or woman had been agonizing in prayer for the salvation of sinners, until the blessing was gained.[8]

In the British 1913 edition of the lectures from which we have just quoted, the editor, W. H. Harding, added this footnote:

The Ulster awakening of 1859 furnishes an apt illustration of this truth. Undoubtedly the circumstances were favourable; earnest preaching of sound doctrine had familiarized the people with, at any rate, a correct theory of the gospel, and the news of the American revival of 1857 had created a spirit of expectancy.

Nevertheless it was from a prayer meeting of obscure and uninfluential young men that the revival—one of the most remarkable ever known in the British Isles—originated. The history of revivals shows again and again how humble believers have prevailed in prayer. *"Homines obscuri"* [obscure men], was the sneering comment of Maitland of Lethington [debating with John Knox] upon a list of preachers. *"Dei tamen servi"* [Servants of God, however], replied Knox.[9]

Second, news of revival movements in other districts and in other countries has often quickened the flame of concern for revival in the hearts of God's people. Accounts of spiritual awakening and advance have inspired other Christians to believe God for His abundant blessing. Claimed G. W. Hervey, "No fact is better established than that the rehearsal of the incidents of other revivals has been of great service in many a work of grace."[10]

Jonathan Edwards stated, "There is no one thing that I know of that God has made such a means of promoting His work among us as the news of others' conversion. This has been owned in awakening sinners, engaging them to seek the same blessing, and in quickening saints."[11]

Hence, there is the supreme and strategic importance of the circulation of books and tracts on the subject of revival. Jonathan Goforth was greatly helped to seek revival for himself through the reading of Finney's *Revival Lectures* and his *Autobiography*.

A third important factor in the birth of revival is Bible-based preaching in the power and unction of the Holy Spirit. While it is not our purpose here to enlarge upon the subject of revival preaching, we would underline the fact stated by David Matthews: "Orthodox theology has always been the hidden source of true revival."[12]

However, it is not the preaching of orthodox theology alone that produces awakening. It is preaching under the anointing of God the Holy Spirit, preaching that, like the Sword of the Spirit, is "quick, and powerful, and sharper than any two-edged sword, piercing even to the dividing asunder of soul and spirit, and of the joints and marrow, and is a discerner of the thoughts and intents of the heart" (Heb 4:12).

WHAT PREVAILS DURING SUCH YEARS OF REVIVAL?

We have considered briefly what spiritual and moral conditions precede revival and what factors precipitate seasons of refreshing. Our third inquiry deals with the *spiritual conditions* that *prevail* during such "years of the right hand of the most High"—that is, we want to learn *the characteristics of revival*.

During a spiritual awakening, there is, first, an overwhelming awareness of the presence of God among His people.

"What have been the outstanding features of this movement?" asked Duncan Campbell of the Lewis revival in the years 1949-1953. "First, an awareness of God."[13] And then he went on to say, "I have no hesitation in saying that this awareness of God is the crying need of the Church today."[14]

19

Next, and this indeed is a sine qua non (essential element) of revival, there is always a profound consciousness and conviction of sin. James Burns wrote,

> Every revival movement sees an awakening of a deep sense of sin in the individual and in the Church. In the intense spiritual light, the sin and guilt of the awakened soul stand out in terrifying blackness.
>
> Not only are the cardinal sins laid bare in all their hideousness, but the convicted see themselves as in a mirror; they see themselves as God sees them; every fault, every meanness, every deviation from the truth, every act of self-interest, of betrayal, of hypocrisy, confronts them. Their sins drag them to judgment; they cry out in their despair; an awful terror seizes them.[15]

"I simply cannot describe the scene," wrote one who passed through such an experience in Manchuria. "It made one think of the Judgment Day. God had come among us. All knew it, and every heart was open before Him. For myself, I had the most intense realization of the holiness of God, and of my uncleanness in His sight."[16]

Third, once sin has been dealt with through confession and the cleansing of the blood of Christ, then believers find their supreme joy in God Himself. (Psalm 85:6—"Wilt thou not revive us again: that thy people may rejoice in thee?")

Dr. Dale, describing the effect produced by Moody and Sankey at the close of their first mission in Birmingham, which produced the deepest impression on the life of the city and its churches, said,

> I hardly know how to describe the change which has passed over them [i.e., the members of his church]. It is like the change which comes upon a landscape where clouds which have been hanging over it for hours suddenly vanish, and the sunlight seems to fill both heaven and earth. There is a joyousness and elasticity of spirit, and a hopefulness, which have completely transformed them.[17]

20

What, then, *proceeds* from such seasons of revival? What are *the results of revival?* In discussing the fourth aspect of these "years of the right hand of the most High," we can do no more than sketch the salient results of revival in a community or country.

First, the spiritual life of the Christian churches in the area is quickened. Men not only have a form of godliness they also have as a result of revival the power thereof. Bible reading and prayer become widespread and meaningful. The devotional life of individuals and families is deepened. Christians enter into a new understanding of the unity that exists among believers in Christ, regardless of denomination or affiliation.

A further result of revival is that the unsaved in the community are reached and brought into a saving relationship to God. Dr. J. Edwin Orr, historian of the 1859 awakening in Britain, stated that as a result of that awakening, one million souls were added to the church.[18]

Also, Christian work in its many forms receives a fresh impetus and increase. Home missions receive the recruits for which there is such a crying need. Thus, the blessing of revival moves out in ever-increasing circles to the ends of the earth.

Finally, the doctrines of the Bible are restored and reaffirmed in all their glorious fullness. "Revival," stated C. E. Autrey, "could prevent theological stagnation. Trends of the times tend to engulf us. We are pressed into certain moulds by the spirit of the age. . . . The greatest contribution of revival today would be at the point of theological need."[19]

WHAT PREVENTS SUCH TIMES OF REVIVAL?

Our final consideration relates personally to the reader. What *prevents* such "years of the right hand of the most High"? What are the *hindrances* to revival?

First, there may be ignorance on the part of the believer. The believer may know little or nothing about the laws of revival or about the history of revival. It is part of the lukewarmness of today that pastors are not systematically teaching their flocks the principles of true revival.

This ignorance, however, cannot be excused, for the Bible itself is the best manual on revival. Let the individual believer "search the Scriptures" for himself with this in mind, and he will discover the laws that govern spiritual awakening.

In addition, there are many books on the subject of revival that will both enlighten and encourage the believer to seek God's face for "years of the right hand of the most High."

Second, where there is a knowledge of the subject of revival, there may exist indifference to the whole matter. Here, surely, is where many of God's people must hang their heads in shame. We have become complacent and cold toward the subject, if not critical. We have little desire to read and to study about the subject of spiritual renewal. We do not stir ourselves to lay hold of God in prayer for revival. There are many reasons that could be given for this sinful indifference, but not one will stand the light of His presence.

Last, and this is the heart of the matter, there is iniquity that like a chain binds the hearts of God's people and with which we are not prepared to part. We are far more eager to excuse sin than to confess it. We remain in our lukewarm condition in spite of the fact that God has warned us that He will spue us out of His mouth (Rev 3:16). "Tell me," said Alan Redpath, "in the light of the Cross, isn't it a scandal that you and I live today as we do?"[20]

We have sought to indicate why revival is needed, how revival is experienced, what revival is, what revival brings, and how revival is hindered. Now, then, what can you do *personally?*

First, become concerned about the need for revival. Shut yourself up with God and carefully review your present spiritual condition. Examine your heart. Do you recognize your need of personal revival?

Second, begin to read about revival. Lay down that popular magazine or that best-selling novel and take up a book on revival. Discipline your reading habits in order to become acquainted with the revival movements of the past.

Third, begin to talk about revival. Make it the subject of your conversation. Talk frequently of the wonderful acts of God (Mal 3:16; Ps 77:12).

Fourth, begin to pray for revival. Come to the mercy seat. Believe God's promises are for you. Cast yourself upon His grace.

Fifth, believe God for a personal revival in your own heart. A young man once asked Gipsy Smith the secret of revival. The great evangelist told him: "Go home. Take a piece of chalk. Draw a circle on the floor around yourself. Then pray: O Lord, revive everything inside this circle."[21]

Could better counsel be given? Our study of the pattern of revival will be eternally profitable only if the reader will here and now pray earnestly for "the years of the right hand of the most High."

REVIVE THY CHURCH

Revive Thy Church, O Living Lord,
And may Thy Spirit be outpoured
Upon all those who long to see
Revival blessing come from Thee.
Oh, hear us, Lord, in this dark hour,
And fill us with Thy Spirit's power!

Revive Thy Church, O Lamb divine,
And cause Thy face on us to shine.
Hast Thou not died our love to win,
And free us from the power of sin?
Oh, break our hearts that we may see
Revival spread abundantly.

Revive Thy Church, O coming King,
The eastern skies are reddening,
And all creation groans and waits
To meet Thee at redemption's gates.
Oh, may Thy bride awake and sing,
Adorned to meet her Bridegroom-King.

TED S. RENDALL

2

THE PHENOMENON OF REVIVAL

And the Lord appeared again in Shiloh: for the Lord revealed himself to Samuel in Shiloh by the word of the Lord. And the word of Samuel came to all Israel. . . . And Samuel spake unto all the house of Israel, saying, If ye do return unto the Lord with all your hearts, then put away the strange gods and Ashtaroth from among you, and prepare your hearts unto the Lord, and serve him only: and he will deliver you out of the hand of the Philistines. Then the children of Israel did put away Baalim and Ashtaroth, and served the Lord only. 1 SAMUEL 3:21—4:1; 7:3-4*

"O LORD, revive thy work in the midst of the years, in the midst of the years make known; in wrath remember mercy" (Hab 3:2).

What did Habakkuk mean by asking the Lord to revive His work in the midst of the years? Here, as in the case of so many of our questions, the Bible is its own best commentary. We say this because in 1 Samuel 1-7 we are given the account of a revival in the nation of Israel, a movement that illustrates for us what it means for the Lord's work to be revived. It is our intention in this study to pinpoint six salient features of the phenomenon of revival and to apply them to our own need in the church today.

THE MILIEU OF REVIVAL

Let us begin by studying the *milieu* of revival, that is, the particular *context* and *circumstances* into which revival comes. By stressing this aspect, we are reminded of the fact that revival does not begin in a vacuum nor does it begin in some ideal setting. Revival comes to a dying church in a decadent society. All of this is illustrated for us in terms of the historical background of the prophet Samuel.

We can begin by focusing on the milieu of revival as it relates to the home. The opening chapters of 1 Samuel have much to say about the decay of the family as a strategic unit in the life of Israel. One family in particular, the family of Eli, is chosen as an illustration and as a warning.

To put it simply yet accurately, there was a generation gap between Eli and his sons. Eli's sons had grown up unchecked and uncontrolled. Speaking concerning the father, the Lord said, "I will judge his house for ever for the iniquity which he knoweth; because his sons made themselves vile, and he restrained them not" (1 Sa 3:13). The marginal reading of that verse suggests that Eli "did not frown upon his sons" (Zondervan ref. ed.).

Eli's sons, therefore, became a law unto themselves and totally disregarded the law of God. It is true that in 1 Samuel 2:22-25 we find Eli reproving his sons, but note that this was when he was an old man (v. 22) and his sons had already established a pattern of immoral, indulgent living. By that time they paid no attention to the moral arguments of their father.

Today we see a complete breakdown in family relationships. The ties that have bound parents and children together in the past are being ruthlessly snapped, and young people are deliberately rejecting the standards and values of their forefathers.

Revival is needed in order to save our families.

With 1 Samuel 1-3 before us, we may also approach the milieu of revival from the standpoint of the church as well as the home.

Eli happened to be the chief priest in the tabernacle system at Shiloh. His sons had been permitted to enter the priesthood, and as Eli became old, they officiated in the matter of the sacrifices. But Eli's sons had introduced "a new morality" into the administration of the offerings and worship of the Lord.

They were guilty, first, of indulgence. They wanted all the choice pieces of meat from the sacrifices for their own tables. They rejected the rights of the Lord and of the offerer and demanded that their physical needs be met first.

They were guilty, second, of immorality. They lived out a Playboy philosophy and sinned sexually with the women "that assembled at the door of the tabernacle of the congregation" (1 Sa 2:22).

Finally, they were guilty of indifference. Too late, Eli did reprove his sons: "Nay, my sons; for it is no good report that I hear: ye make the Lord's people to transgress" (v. 24). In spite of Eli's reproof, his sons "hearkened not unto the voice of their father" (v. 25).

We are in no way stretching the point to say that these conditions are being repeated in the church today. There are men in positions of leadership in the church who covet power and position. They are concerned only about their own preservation and promotion.

There are men in the church today guilty of disregarding the moral laws of God and of openly advocating a new morality, where sexual indulgence either before marriage or outside marriage is condoned.

In spite of the teachings and warnings of God's Word, such leaders continue in their chosen path with no brokenness or repentance, "blind leaders of the blind" who have no compassion for the people whom they cause to transgress.

Besides learning something about family life and church life as we study the milieu of revival in Samuel's day, we may learn something about the nation of Israel. Because of the failure of the home and the failure of the church, Israel as a nation was in a serious condition.

Israel had been defiled by her idolatry. Samuel alludes to this in his appeal to Israel. He refers to the "strange gods" and to Ashtaroth, that is, the deities of the Canaanites, which the people of Israel had begun to worship. As a result, Israel had been polluted morally and spiritually. The peope had become unfaithful to Jehovah, their loving Lord who had brought them out of Egypt and into the land of Palestine.

Israel had been defeated by her enemies. The parenthetical section, 1 Samuel 4:1—7:2, explains the military defeat of Israel and shows us a people out of touch with God, trusting in the ark of the Lord rather than in the Lord of the ark and being soundly trounced on the battlefield by the Philistines.

Put all these factors together, and we have a picture of a nation on the rocks, a nation at the end of its tether: its family life ruined, its religious life a farce, and its national spirit broken. These circumstances have been repeated again and again in the history of nations, and repeatedly revival has come to nations at the darkest hour—morally, spiritually, ethically, and politically—of their existence.

Let us never in unbelief say that our circumstances are too hard for God. Let us never imagine that our times are worse than any times previous in the history of the church. Let us believe God and His Word.

THE MEANING OF REVIVAL

But what is the *meaning* of revival? The term is often used loosely, without a true awareness of its rich significance and its strategic importance.

As we study the selected Scriptures from 1 Samuel, we learn that revival means at least three basic things.

First, revival means a fresh communication of God's Word. During the early life of Samuel, "the word of the Lord was precious," that is, rare. "There was no open vision" (1 Sa 3:1). But God's hand was upon Samuel, and His message was in his mouth so that "all Israel from Dan even to Beersheba knew that Samuel was established to be a prophet of the Lord" (v. 20). Here, then, is a leading characteristic of revival. God's Word speaks in living, contemporary, authoritative tones. It is true that Israel had the law, but they needed a Spirit-anointed interpreter of that law in the office of prophet, and Samuel was God's man for that need.

Second, according to 1 Samuel 3:21, revival involves a fresh consciousness of God's presence with His people. "And the Lord appeared again in Shiloh: for the Lord revealed Himself to Samuel in Shiloh by the word of the Lord." In revival God manifests Himself as the living God. His people have sudden—and sometimes startling—revelations of His holiness and righteousness and grace. But it is the Lord *Himself* who engages the affections and attention of His people. Any movement where the Lord is not central, where He is not worshiped and adored, is subbiblical in its emphasis.

Third, according to 1 Samuel 7:4, revival includes as well a fresh commitment to God's holy and just requirements. "Then the children of Israel did put away Baalim and Ashtaroth, and served the Lord only." We would stress the word *only.* Hitherto they had worshiped Jehovah along with the idols of the pagans. But God's solemn requirement was, "Thou shalt have no other gods before me" (Ex 20:3). Revival sees a fresh commitment to God alone. We exalt Him alone as our God and enthrone Him alone as our King.

THE MEDIUM OF REVIVAL

Our selected Scripture from 1 Samuel indicates to us in no uncertain terms what the *medium* of revival is. "The Lord revealed himself to Samuel in Shiloh by the word of the LORD" (1 Sa 3:21). It was that word which Samuel in turn communicated to Israel: "And the word of Samuel came to all Israel" (4:1).

Jonathan Goforth, greatly used of the Spirit of God in spiritual awakenings, said categorically, "The Sword of the Spirit, which is the Word of God, is the only weapon which has ever been mightily used in revival."[1]

In revival, God's Word is seen to be truly divine. It is seen as the Sword of the Spirit par excellence. It has no rival in its ability to probe and pierce the hearts of men and women. In times of awakening, that Word is most highly prized as being the Word of God.

Accordingly in revival, God's Word is seen to be truly dynamic. Hearts that have resisted the sermons and speeches of pastors and evangelists are suddenly broken by the hammer of the Spirit. A phrase or a sentence from the Scriptures has broken down all resistance and brought the repentant heart to the feet of God for forgiveness and freedom.

In revival, God's Word is seen to be a Word speaking in definite terms to His people today. When God's Word is interpreted by cold-hearted hermeneutics, its basic meaning may, indeed, be given correctly, but its personal application is generally set aside. The interpreter claims he does not want to use the passage out of context or to misapply God's Word. But in times of revival, the Holy Spirit makes His own application of His Word to hearts. God's Word becomes His Word to me personally, definitely, directly.

THE MESSAGE OF REVIVAL

What, then, is the *message* of revival? What is its content? The brief summary of Samuel's message, given to us in 1 Samuel 7:3, outlines the message of revival.

First, Samuel indicates the nature of revival. "If ye do return unto the Lord with all your hearts—" Returning to the

Lord is the essence of revival. Sin involves desertion from the Lord; revival involves the decision to return to the Lord. Samuel's added words, "with all your hearts," teach us that, in returning to the Lord, we must be wholehearted, not half hearted. Then Samuel indicates the conditions of revival. "If ye do return unto the Lord with all your hearts, then put away the strange gods and Ashtaroth from among you, and prepare your hearts unto the Lord, and serve Him only." The conditions are simple, demanding personal and immediate and wholehearted obedience.

Finally, Samuel indicates the promise of revival. "If ye do return unto the Lord with all your hearts, then put away strange gods and Ashtaroth from among you, and prepare your hearts unto the Lord, and serve him only: and he will deliver you out of the hand of the Philistines." God is prepared to intervene on behalf of His people in their plight if they will respond to His demands. Deliverance is at the end of the road of obedience.

The message of revival is never stereotyped, but it always includes certain essentials. There will be an emphasis upon the nature of revival itself. There will be a presentation of the conditions of revival. And there will be a proclamation of the promises that God had made to those who return to Him.

THE MARKS OF REVIVAL

When Israel responded to Samuel's message and "put away Baalim and Ashtaroth, and served the Lord only," Samuel arranged for a special meeting at Mizpeh. This meeting is described in 1 Samuel 7:5-12, and as we read the passage, we discover the *marks* of true revival.

First, there was confession of sin. "They gathered together to Mizpeh, and drew water, and poured it out before the Lord, and fasted on that day, and said there, We have sinned against the Lord" (7:6). This is followed by the statement: "And Samuel judged the children of Israel in Mizpeh." Does that suggest that Samuel had to settle various matters that were brought to him as a result of the broken hearts of God's people? Samuel became counselor to his people.

Second, there was confidence in God. The Philistines heard about the mass meeting at Mizpeh and, supposing that the people of Israel were assembling for war, sent an army against them. Faced by the enemy, the people of Israel now put their confidence in the Lord: "And the children of Israel said to Samuel, Cease not to cry unto the LORD our God for us, that he will save us out of the hand of the Philistines" (7:8).

With such confidence in God, there was, of course, victory over their enemies. As Samuel offered a sacrifice to the Lord, a symbol of Israel's devotion to and dependence upon the Lord, "The LORD thundered with a great thunder on that day upon the Philistines, and discomfited them; and they were smitten before Israel" (7:10). No enemy can withstand the church when she is revived. Then she becomes truly the church militant.

Finally, we note that there was praise to God. After the victory, "Samuel took a stone, and set it between Mizpeh and Shen, and called the name of it Eben-ezer, saying, Hitherto hath the LORD helped us" (7:12). Here is the acknowledgment that Jehovah is the Lord who intervenes in times of crisis. Samuel's stone was a monument to God's faithfulness.

THE MIRACLE OF REVIVAL

We bring this study to a close by reminding ourselves once again of the miracle—indeed, mystery—of revival. God is the God of revival, and He is the God of wonders. He brings life out of death, light out of darkness, deliverance out of defeat, blessing out of backsliding. He transforms the wilderness into a garden and converts the desert into an irrigated land. That is the miracle of revival.

When God is at work, then, we may expect the unusual; we may see the "impossible"; we may share in the new thing of God's grace. Problems that have defied solution for years are resolved; situations that have resisted change are transformed; tensions that have built up over a period of time are eased. Despair gives way to hope, pessimism gives way to a glorious optimism in the Lord, fear gives way to courage and confidence in the Lord.

With this account before us, we should pray with Habakkuk: "O Lord, revive thy work in the midst of the years, in the midst of the years make known; in wrath remember mercy."

Revive Thy work—revive us—revive me!

PRAYER FOR REVIVAL

Revive Me   Psalm 138:7

My love is cold, my faith is small,
My zeal is lacking, doubts appal;
My footsteps falter, oft I stray,
And weakness marks me for its prey:
Empower, endue, revive e'en me.

Revive Us   Psalm 85:6

With all Thine own in Jesus' name,
We would confess our common shame,
And humbly bow before Thy face
To seek Thy pardoning, cleansing grace:
God of revival, God of love,
Refresh, revive us from above.

Revive Thy Work   Habakkuk 3:2

Thy workers' hearts are filled with dread,
The lost are left, Thy sheep unfed,
Thine enemies Thy work defy,
And things are weak, ready to die:
God of revival, now we pray,
Visit Thy work in this our day.

They Shall Revive   Hosea 14:7

Oh, for Thy Spirit's quickening breath!
Reviving from the sleep of death;
Oh, for Thy mighty ancient power!
Arousing us this very hour:
God of revival, Thee we praise
For signs of blessing in our days.

AUTHOR UNKNOWN

3

THE POSSIBILITY OF REVIVAL

*If I shut up heaven that there be no rain, or if I
command the locusts to devour the land, or if I
send pestilence among my people: if my people,
which are called by my name, shall humble themselves, and pray, and seek my face, and turn from
their wicked ways; then will I hear from heaven,
and will forgive their sins, and will heal their land.*
2 CHRONICLES 7:13-14.

"REVIVAL IN OUR TIME." For over a decade this simple
slogan has set forth the deepest desire of many Christians.
None will dare to deny or dispute the fact that spiritual revival is desperately needed among God's people. And yet, as
we examine the condition of the church today, we are forced
to ask ourselves the question, What are the possibilities of
seeing revival in our time? In other words, how can the
earnest desire expressed in the slogan be realized? Is there
scriptural justification for believing that revival is not just a
phenomenon of the past but the glorious possibility of the
present?

Without doubt, the verses most often quoted in reference
to revival in our time are 2 Chronicles 7:13-14. This portion
of Jehovah's message to Solomon at the dedication of the
temple forms the classical reference for the subject of revival.

Some, zealous for dispensational distinctions, will immediately point out that the passage has no bearing whatsoever on
the condition of the church today and that what is in view

in these verses is the restoration of Israel after a period of backsliding. Therefore, they claim, we have no right to discuss the subject of revival using these verses as our basis.

While we grant the fact that the verses relate directly to Israel in the land, we are not prepared to concede that, therefore, they can have nothing to say to the church of today. There are abiding principles in every dispensation, and because we may trace a very definite analogy between Israel and the church, we may relate accordingly some of the aspects of this passage to the spiritual realm.

What, then, do these verses have to say to the church in the space age?

The Existing Situation that Precedes Revival

The verses are of great value in that they pinpoint and portray the existing situation that precedes revival. Basic to the thought of revival is the fact of barrenness, of ruin, of backsliding. These verses clearly speak of just such conditions. They remind us forcibly of the fact that revival is essential because of the plight and predicament of God's people. Let us analyze the conditions as here indicated and apply them to our own day.

In His message to Solomon, the Lord spoke first of a heaven shut up. "If I shut up heaven that there be no rain—" The reference is to the copious showers of Palestine being withheld as an act of divine judgment upon Israel. The result of such withholding of the showers (Jer 3:3), of course, would be deadly drought and fearful famine and waterless wells.

Palestine, the land of promise, was described by Moses as "a land of hills and valleys, and drinketh water of the rain of heaven" (Deu 11:11). It is hardly necessary to emphasize the importance of rain to a people whose way of life was largely agricultural and who, therefore, depended largely upon the produce of the land for sustenance.

36

Now, just as the presence of rain was regarded as a special sign of God's blessing and favor, so the absence of rain was interpreted as a sign of God's judgment and disfavor. Thus Moses predicted a time when "The heaven that is over thy head shall be brass, and the earth that is under thee shall be iron. The Lord shall make the rain of thy land powder and dust: from heaven shall it come down upon thee, until thou be destroyed" (Deu 28:23-24). The land of Palestine would become a dust bowl, a veritable disaster area.

And why? Why would God shut up the heaven? Why would He withhold the showers? The answer is clear and certain. Solomon understood why. In 2 Chronicles 6:26, he prayed, "When the heaven is shut up, and there is no rain, because they have sinned against thee—"

"Because they have sinned against thee"—that was the explanation of the shut and sealed and silent heaven. That was the reason for showers withheld, for drought, for famine, for misery. The reason lay in the people's relationship to God. They had sinned against Him.

Now a time of spiritual declension in the church may be spoken of as a time of "no rain," and, on the other hand, a time of revival may be described as a time of "showers of blessing" (Eze 34:26). Indeed, this imagery has become part of the songs we sing. For instance:

> Oh, for the showers on the thirsty land!
> Oh, for a mighty revival!
> Oh, for a sanctified, fearless band,
> Ready to hail its arrival!
>
> W. LESLIE

And another song proclaims:

> There shall be showers of blessing;
> This is the promise of love;

37

There shall be seasons refreshing
Sent from the Saviour above.

DANIEL W. WHITTLE

In Israel, the rain of heaven was withheld from fields and vineyards. In the church, God's fructifying blessing is withheld from the sown seed, which is the Word of God. Why? In both cases, the answer is the same—sin in the hearts of God's people. Let us not seek to shift the blame to present-day conditions—the hardness of men's hearts, greedy materialism, the international conflict, the moral chaos. Let us face the fact in honesty and humiliation—The reason for the shut heaven is the sin of God's people.

But there is indicated here a second aspect to the condition that precedes revival, and this is given to us in the words, "If I command the locusts to devour the land." Here the reference is to plagues of locusts, greedily devouring every green thing in the land and leaving nothing but desolation in their wake. Such swarms of locusts were greatly feared by the people, who were utterly defenseless before the marauding hosts. The prophet Joel has given us a vivid description of the effects of such a plague. So unparalleled was it in its destruction and devastation that he called upon the people of Israel: "Hear this, ye old men, and give ear, all ye inhabitants of the land. Hath this been in your days, or even in the days of your fathers?" (Joel 1:2).

Now let us name some of the "locusts" that are devouring the church.

There is the locust we call materialism. Here is an enemy that is presently plaguing the church. Today materialism has been exalted to the rank of a god, and multitudes are bowing before its shrine. Material things have become an end in themselves, rather than a means to an end: the publication of the good news of salvation. Far too many Christians cannot give as they ought to give to the Lord's work because they have

38

many commitments financially, often for things that do not come in the class of necessities, but of luxuries. Surely of this enemy the Lord may say, "He hath laid my vine waste, and barked my fig tree: he hath made it clean bare, and cast it away; the branches thereof are made white" (Joel 1:7).

Second, in the political world there is the locust of Communism. It has devoured great stretches of the world, and, in the course of its cruel conquest, has trodden down the Christian church. "A nation is come upon my land, strong, and without number, whose teeth are the teeth of a lion, and he hath the cheek teeth of a great lion" (Joel 1:6). While in God's mercy a remnant has been spared, nevertheless, the church has not been able to prosper and propagate in countries overrun by Communism.

Third, in the religious world there is the locust of modernism. For nearly a century, modernism has been plaguing the Christian church. Joel 1:4 is an instructive verse concerning the varieties of the locust plague. "That which the palmerworm hath left hath the locust eaten; and that which the locust hath left hath the cankerworm eaten; and that which the cankerworm hath left hath the caterpillar eaten." These successive plagues had devastated the land.

The evolution of modernism in the Christian church has had a similar pattern of development and a similar work of destruction. The plague has been called modernism, liberalism, and now neoorthodoxy. By whatever name it is called, there is still in it the same tendency that is destructive of the faith delivered to the saints. The plague is still attempting to destroy the inspiration and authority of Scripture, the incarnation and virgin birth of Christ, and other fundamental doctrines, "trees in the house of the Lord."

We should remind ourselves at this point that the locusts in the land of Israel were sent by the Lord. They were sent as a judgment upon God's people, "If I command the locusts to devour the land," God said. God is sovereign in judgment, and if His people sin against Him, He uses scourges to drive them to repentance. Thus He accomplishes His purposes.

The third aspect of the condition that precedes revival is summed up in the words, "If I send pestilence among my people." This is amplified for us in Deuteronomy 28:58-59: "If thou wilt not observe to do all the words of this law that are written in this book, that thou mayest fear his glorious and fearful name, THE LORD THY GOD; Then the Lord will make thy plagues wonderful, and the plagues of thy seed, even great plagues, and of long continuance, and sore sicknesses, and of long continuance."

"Pestilence among my people." Can we identify such among God's people today?

Definitely there can be found among God's people today a serious ophthalmic condition, the result of which is spiritual blindness. In some, this plague has been of "long continuance." In others, the disease has not yet fully taken its course, the symptoms being dimness of sight or possibly a distortion of true spiritual values. To a church suffering from this pestilence the Lord Jesus said, "I counsel thee to . . . anoint thine eyes with eyesalve, that thou mayest see" (Rev 3:18).

There is, too, an acute knee trouble afflicting many of God's saints. In such cases the ailment is so chronic that the sufferers cannot bend their knees in prayer; indeed, they have little desire to do so. They cannot join with the apostle Paul in saying, "I bow my knees unto the Father of our Lord Jesus Christ" (Eph 3:14); nor can they join with Daniel and a host of other Bible saints who daily bowed their knees in worship and prayer.

There is also a widespread hearing ailment among God's people. They cannot hear what the Spirit is saying to the churches (Rev 2:7). A strange feature of the sickness is that the patient can hear what people are saying but cannot hear what God is saying. These need to pray with Solomon for a "hearing heart" (1 Ki 3:9, Zondervan ref. ed., marg.)

Many, too, suffer constantly from a serious neck condition, better known as stiff neck. This shows up in a spirit of independence and obstinacy so characteristic of babes in Christ. Of Israel it is written, "They obeyed not, neither inclined their ear, but made their neck stiff, that they might not hear, nor receive instruction" (Jer 17:23).

Above all, many of God's saints are suffering from a heart condition, variously described in the Word of God. Some have a "double heart" (Ps 12:2); others have a proud heart (Ps 101:5). Some have a lukewarm heart, making their love for God neither fervent nor frigid.

These are some of the pestilences prevalent among God's people, divinely permitted for a specific purpose: to awaken us to a sense of our need that we may call upon the Lord to heal the affliction of our souls.

The Essential Steps that Promote Revival

We have considered in some detail the existing situation that precedes revival. We have seen that before a revival, heaven is shut up, plagues are let loose, and pestilences are prevalent among God's people. With these conditions as a background, let us now consider the essential steps that promote revival in our midst. They are four in number, and taken together, they remind us that *revival is conditional.* We would not stress any one step as having priority, inasmuch as when one step is truly taken, the believer is committed to walk the way of revival.

"If my people," said Jehovah to Solomon, "which are called by my name, shall humble themselves—" Before blessing, therefore, there must be brokenness.

What is involved in such humbling of ourselves?

We stress first the confession of God's majesty and glory. Man is humbled only as he sees the person and purity and power of God. This may be traced in various prayers of saints in the Bible. (E.g., Neh 9:5-38; Jer 32:17-25; Dan 9:3-19)

This is the reason the exposition of the law of God as the expression of God's character and claims, in all its depth and height and length and breadth, has often preceded times of revival. As the permanent and paramount features of the holy law of God have been heralded, men and women, like Isaiah, have seen the Lord, high and lifted up. "Some say that they are gospel preachers," said John Wesley; "I am a law and gospel preacher."[1]

But, hand in hand, with the confession of God's might and majesty, there must be the admission of man's weakness and wickedness. Indeed, this is simply the corollary of the first. Isaiah saw God's glory; he then saw his own guilt. Peter exhorted believers to "humble yourselves therefore under the mighty hand of God" (1 Pe 5:6).

But the second step is just as vital, just as necessary, just as urgent. Brokenness must be accompanied by prayer. It is prayer that gives expression to our inmost desires. Prayer articulates the need of the soul.

Is it necessary to enlarge upon this theme? Such prayer must be believing prayer. It must be definite prayer. It must be fervent prayer. We need add no more. Let us pray.

The third step reminds us that a holy God cannot look upon sin, and He, therefore, turns away from those who sin, an act and attitude indicating His displeasure.

"When thou saidst, Seek ye my face; my heart said unto thee, thy face, Lord, will I seek" (Ps 27:8). "Let the heart of them rejoice that seek the Lord. Seek the Lord, and his strength: seek his face evermore" (Ps 105:3-4). With such encouragements, let us seek the Lord while He may be found.

The fourth step is to turn from our wicked ways, ways of deceit, of unrighteousness, of impurity, of worldliness, of ungodliness. This is the final proof that the humbling of ourselves has been real, that our prayer has been sincere, and that our seeking His face has been genuine. If we are drawn closer to the throne of His majesty, our sin will appear hideous and loathsome; if our prayer for His blessing has been from a pure heart, we shall abhor that which has brought His disfavor upon us; if we have truly sought His face initially, we shall not seek to continue any longer in the paths of unrighteousness.

What word could better describe the change that is demanded than the verb, *turn?* True repentance involves a complete reversal of one's former way of life. It issues in a thorough revolution.

THE ENCOURAGING STATEMENT THAT PROMISES REVIVAL

But have we any assurance that when these steps are taken we shall see revival in our time? We have just outlined the steps that promote revival; now consider the encouraging statement that promises revival. "Then will I hear from heaven, and will forgive their sin, and will heal their land."

Here is a threefold promise:

First, if and when God's people take the steps, God will hear from heaven. "Then will I hear from heaven." God will respond to His people's cry. This is His Word to us. His hearing of our cry assures us of an answer. He will hear us favorably and will initiate a program of divine blessing. The shut heaven will be opened to the cry of faith.

Second, God promises to forgive our sin. "Then . . . will [I] forgive their sins." Before God can favor His people, He must forgive their sin. Before revival, there must be remission of sin. "There is forgiveness with thee," cried the psalmist, "that thou mayest be feared."

The third aspect of this encouraging statement assures God's people of His blessing upon their land. In Israel's case, God promised to restore prosperity to their land. This meant fields of golden grain, fruitful vineyards and gardens—all of this and more. No longer would there be plagues and pestilences. Throughout the land, God's smile would be seen.

43

Let the people of the land get right with God; then the land of the people is blessed by God. Revival brings in its train a host of blessings: national, social, moral, and educational. This is the promise of God.

"Revival in our time"—is it possible? In the light of the teaching of Scripture, we answer yes. A Chinese proverb reminds us, however, that he who would take a thousand steps must take the first one. Let us take the first step *now*. As Leonard Ravenhill assures us, "Revival can be brought to this generation by prayer, by faith, by cleansing, and by obedience to the will of God."[2]

CHRIST IS ON THE THRONE

We are praying for revival for the land is sere and dry;
We are praying for revival, till the showers come from on
    high;
And a whisper comes to strengthen us, Pray on, pray on, 'tis
    nigh;
      For Christ is on the throne.
We are digging deep the ditches though no wind or rain we
    see;
We are breaking up the fallow ground that ready it may be.
By the standard of the Spirit Satan's host are made to flee;
      For Christ is on the throne.

We are praying for the fire from Elijah's God today;
We are praying for the idols to be burnt up as its prey;
We are longing for our Jesus to be magnified alway,
      The Christ upon the throne.

We are praying for the showers of the blessed latter rain;
We expect to see the harvest of abundant golden grain;
For He promised to send floods upon the dry and thirsty
    plain;
      And Christ is on the throne.
We are looking to God's storehouse and the tithes we're
    bringing in;
We are learning to abhor the awful sinfulness of sin;
We are praising for the precious Blood that cleanses all
    within;
      For Christ is on the throne.
We have launched into the river at the Lord our God's com-
    mand;
He has cut away our shorelines by His own almighty hand;
A multitude of fish we'll bring in for Emmanuel's Land;
      For Christ is on the throne.

AUTHOR UNKNOWN

4

THE PROMISE OF REVIVAL

Remember ye not the former things, neither consider the things of old. Behold, I will do a new thing; now it shall spring forth; shall ye not know it? I will even make a way in the wilderness, and rivers in the desert. The beast of the field shall honour me, the dragons and the owls: because I give waters in the wilderness, and rivers in the desert, to give drink to my people, my chosen. This people have I formed for myself; they shall shew forth my praise. ISAIAH 43:18-21

"BEHOLD, I WILL DO a new thing."

This glorious and golden promise was initially given to the people of Israel as that nation faced the prospect of the Babylonian captivity. These words predicted and pledged for the last days a "new thing," a new work, a new miracle, on Israel's behalf. Jehovah will intervene in mercy and might on behalf of His captive people. As a result, there will be release and restoration and the consequent realization of God's purpose for His people.

We reckon and rejoice that in God's time, in accordance with God's clock of the ages, this promise will be fulfilled in relation to the elect nation of Israel. We believe that there is a day coming when God will intervene on behalf of His chosen people and manifest His grace and glory to them. In that day all of God's great purposes relative to Israel will be consummated and completed.

47

But having said that, we may apply this promise to ourselves without in any way distorting the inner meaning of the passage. God is the same yesterday, today, and forever, and He waits to work His new thing in our age as well as in other dispensations. His desire and His declaration remain the same. Thus, we may confidently learn from these verses what God's "new thing" for our age actually is.

As we face the terms and truths of this passage, three inquiries with regard to God's new thing press themselves upon us.

RELATING GOD'S NEW THING

First, we must ask *how we are to relate this new work to the past.*

We raise this question because of the divine command in Isaiah 43:18, "Remember ye not the former things, neither consider the things of old." On the surface, this appears to be a command to shut our eyes completely to the events and experiences of the past and to close forever the pages of the book of history. But is this what is meant? That there is a very definite value in studying the past is an incontrovertible fact. Indeed, in the very same book from which our text is taken, we read another divine command: "Remember the former things of old: for I am God, and there is none else" (Is 46:9).

In the light of these considerations, we must determine precisely how we are to relate God's new thing on behalf of His people to what He has done in the past.

We begin by affirming that this new thing does not involve any change in God Himself. "I am the LORD," is His claim, "I change not" (Mal 3:6). And what that meant practically to Israel is clearly expressed in Isaiah 43:15: "I am the LORD, your Holy One, the creator of Israel, your King." In that verse His leading attributes are stressed, attributes which are eternal.

With regard, therefore, to His new work on behalf of His people, we should firmly grasp the fact that such a new thing does not involve any change in God Himself. This new thing involves no new doctrine of God nor any startling discovery about God. Many in our time resemble the Athenians of old who "spent their time in nothing else, but either to tell, or to hear some new thing" (Ac 17:21).

But we may be certain of this, that God's new thing is in no way related to the empty speculations of modern theologians or to the ridiculous reasonings of modern philosophers. God has revealed His nature and person in the Scriptures, and His new thing will ever be in accord with that revelation of Himself.

Second, and this follows from our first observation, this new thing promised by God involves no basic change in His Word. That Word, like Him who spoke it, is forever settled in heaven. That Word is subject to no alterations or additions.

We are mistaken, therefore, if we are constantly looking for some new message, some novel interpretation, some radical exposition that somehow will do for us what God's written Word in its simple meaning will not accomplish in our hearts. We recognize, of course, that God will constantly give more light as to the understanding of His Word. He will send out His light and His truth, but this involves no change in that Word itself; rather, it is our understanding of that Word which is deepened and enlarged and increased.

Again, we may state that God's new thing does not involve any new or novel emphasis upon our need and our condition before Him. The need of men and women remains the same in every age; it may assume a multitude of forms. It may display itself in a hundred different ways. But that need, as to its essence, is constant. Men need the grace of God. They need forgiveness and deliverance from sin. They need redemption and release.

This, too, is the constant need of the church. God's people

today need to be delivered from captivity. For too long they have been manacled by the world, victims of its spirit, slaves to its fashions. God's people need, too, God's pardon and forgiveness. They need to know the grace of God in cleansing and purification. God's new thing does not ignore these needs of men and women.

Finally, we may state that this divine new thing involves no minimizing or overlooking what God has done in the past. To study how God has revealed Himself in His Word, to become aware of His working in the past, to see how God has met His people in their need—this is all profitable for the believer.

How, then, are we to interpret the command of Isaiah 43:18, "Remember ye not the former things, neither consider the things of old"? Surely this command is to be interpreted along the following line. God's people are exhorted not to live, as it were, in the past. We are not to be dwelling among the tombs of the illustrious dead—for Israel—Moses, David, Elijah; for us—Jonathan Edwards, John Wesley, Charles Finney.

One of the dangers of reading the records of revivals and the biographies of revival leaders lies in the subtle idea that God's activity is confined to the past. We may even begin to reason that God, if He intervenes today in the reviving of His people, must work precisely in the manner as He did in past revivals.

But we are not to be geared to the past. We are to be living in the present. Our faith must be in the living God. We are to be concerned primarily with what God is able to do today.

A wonderful commentary on God's new thing for His people Israel is found in Jeremiah 23:7-8. We read: "The days come, saith the LORD, that they shall no more say, The Lord liveth, which brought up the children of Israel out of the land of Egypt; but, The LORD liveth, which brought up and which led the seed of the house of Israel out of the north country, and from all countries whither I had driven them."

That is relating God's new thing properly to the past.

In summary, therefore, we may state that God's new thing involves no change in God Himself or in His Word or in our need. The command to forget the past must, then, be interpreted as a command to live not in the past but in the present.

RECOGNIZING GOD'S NEW THING

We turn now to consider a second urgent question. How are we to recognize God's new thing for our age? Is it possible for us to indicate the traits of this new triumph?

We believe that the chapter from which our text is taken outlines the basic aspects of God's new thing, and by these, in turn, we may recognize His working in the hearts of His people.

First, this new thing involves a fresh adoration of the Lord's person.

We find this emphasis in a number of the verses of Isaiah 43. In 43:3 we read, "I am the LORD thy God, the Holy One of Israel, thy Saviour." Again, in 43:11 we read, "I, even I, am the LORD; and beside me there is no saviour." The same note is expressed in 43:14, "The LORD, your redeemer, the Holy One of Israel." It is found, too, in 43:15, "I am the LORD, your Holy One, the creator of Israel, your King." And it occurs again in 43:25, "I, even I, am He that blotteth out thy trangressions for mine own sake."

Jehovah is Israel's Creator and Saviour. He is supreme and holy and gracious. He rules and redeems and forgives His people. What a contrast to the idols and the gods worshiped by the Babylonians! We need to remember that Isaiah's message was designed to enlighten and encourage the people of Israel as they underwent the Babylonian captivity. There in Babylon they were surrounded by idols "profitable for nothing" (Is 44:10).

51

In contrast with these idols, the God of Israel was alive and active and identified with His people in their need. And God's new thing on behalf of His people will result in His people coming to know Him as their Ruler and Redeemer.

We may unequivocally state, therefore, that the hallmark of God's new thing is a fresh adoration of the Lord's person. Any message or movement that does not bring God's people to their knees in worship and adoration is shallow and superficial. So definitely is this a mark of God's moving among His people that the prophet declares that even the beasts of the field and the birds of the air will honor Jehovah!

But God's new thing involves next a fresh appropriation of the Lord's provision.

Here is the prophetic announcement: "Behold, I will do a new thing: . . . I will even make a way in the wilderness, and rivers in the desert. . . . I give waters in the wilderness, and rivers in the desert, to give drink to my people, my chosen."

God's people will appropriate God's way, "a way in the wilderness," and God's waters, "rivers in the desert."

God's way is a highway and is called "the way of holiness" (Is 35:8). It is a way barred to the unclean. "No lion shall be there, nor any ravenous beast shall go up thereon, it shall not be found there; but the redeemed shall walk there" (35:9).

God's new thing will thus provide direction for His people. There will be an end to our aimlessness and wanderings. God promises His people: "I will cause them to walk by the rivers of waters in a straight way, wherein they shall not stumble" (Jer 31:9). "Set thine heart," therefore, "toward the highway" (31:21).

God's waters are abundant and refreshing, available to all who walk the way of holiness. In accordance with God's promise, "In the wilderness shall waters break out, and streams in the desert. And the parched ground shall become a pool, and the thirsty land springs of water" (Is 35:6-7).

When God's new thing for our age is introduced, God's people will appropriate afresh the Lord's provision.

Finally, we may note that when God's new thing is experienced by God's people there will be a fresh apprehension on our part of the Lord's purpose. "This people," declares the God of the new thing, "have I formed for myself; they shall shew forth my praise."

Peter echoes the divine word here when he writes: "Ye are a chosen generation, a royal priesthood, an holy nation, a peculiar people; that ye should shew forth the praises of him who hath called you out of darkness into His marvellous light" (1 Pe 2:9).

The Lord's purpose is that His people "advertise" His praise. Daily in our lives this purpose should be fulfilled; yet how often we fail to show forth His praise! God's new thing will see this purpose achieved.

Realizing God's New Thing

Our third inquiry, therefore, must relate to this achieving of God's purpose. We must discover how God's new thing may be realized and effected in our time.

Here again, Isaiah 43 presents clearly the way in which God's new thing may be experienced. First, there must be a looking away from circumstances to God. In Isaiah 43:2, Israel's captivity is described figuratively as a passing through flood waters, as a walking through fierce fires. But Israel is not to look at her environment or at her circumstances. She must look to God, to the Lord that created the nation, her Saviour and King (43:3, 14-15).

Second, there must be faith in God and in His power to intervene. "Ye are my witnesses, saith the Lord, and my servant whom I have chosen: that ye may know and believe me, and understand that I am he" (43:10). Christians must believe that He is able to accomplish His purposes: "I will work, and who shall turn it back?" (43:13, Zondervan ref. ed. marg.). Unbelief with regard to this will assuredly rob us of God's new thing.

Third, there must be calling upon God. In 43:22, God accuses Israel of not calling upon Him. "Thou hast not called upon me, O Jacob; but thou hast been weary of me, O Israel."

How tragic that God's people refuse to call upon Him in prayer! Yet God's new thing comes only in answer to their prayers. When God's people are in captivity, that is, when they are where they should not be, where they are not able to fulfill God's purpose for them, then they need God's new thing to bring redemption and deliverance, but they must call upon Him in sincerity and in truth.

What are the prospects for revival? That question was once put to an old saint. His answer? "As bright as the promises of God." We have seen from this passage that God promises a new thing for our age; let us lay hold of the promise by faith and see Him work on behalf of His people today.

AWAKE THOU SPIRIT

Awake, Thou Spirit, who of old
Didst fire the watchmen of the Church's youth;
Who faced the foe, unshrinking, bold,
Who witnessed day and night the eternal truth,
Whose voices through the world are ringing still,
And bringing hosts to know and do Thy will.

Oh that Thy fire were kindled soon,
That swift from land to land its flame might leap;
Lord, give us but this priceless boon
Of faithful servants, fit for Thee to reap
The harvest of the soul; look down and view
How great the harvest, yet the labourers few.

Would there were help within our walls!
Oh, let Thy promised Spirit come again,
Before whom every barrier falls,
And, ere the night, once more shine forth as then!
Oh, rend the heavens, and make Thy presence felt;
The chains that bind us at Thy touch would melt!

And let Thy Word have speedy course,
Through every land the truth be glorified,
Till all the heathen know its force,
And gather to Thy churches far and wide;
And waken Israel from her sleep, O Lord!
Thus bless and spread the conquests of Thy Word!

The Church's desert paths restore,
That stumbling blocks, which long in them have lain,
May hinder now Thy Word no more;
Destroy false doctrine, root out notions vain;
Set free from hirelings, let the church and school
Bloom as a garden 'neath Thy prospering rule!

BOGATZKY

5

THE PRAYER FOR REVIVAL

Oh that thou wouldest rend the heavens, that thou wouldest come down, that the mountains might flow down at thy presence, as when the melting fire burneth, the fire causeth the waters to boil, to make thy name known to thine adversaries, that the nations may tremble at thy presence! When thou didst terrible things which we looked not for, thou camest down, the mountains flowed down at thy presence. ISAIAH 64:1-3

WHY IS THE REVIVAL God's people desire so long in coming? Why is it that with conditions in our land as desperate as they are—socially, morally, spiritually—we do not see the flame of revival burning in the hearts of all true believers? Why do we not see in our day as our forefathers saw in their "days of heaven upon earth"? These are basic and urgent questions—questions that must be faced by us honestly and humbly if we are to locate the source of the church's present impoverishment and impotency.

This problem of an unrevived church is being approached in various ways. Some believe that the disunity that exists among evangelical Christians is the major cause of the church's present condition. They argue that if all believers would seek to foster and promote our unity in Christ, then we would see a real measure of revival blessing poured out upon us. Others point to the church's criminal failure in her high and holy calling of world evangelization. They assure us that if the church will "go into all the world and preach the gospel," there will be, as a result, "times of refreshing from the presence of the Lord."

Again, there are those who are convinced that God's blessing is withheld because the church has robbed God of tithes and offerings. They assert that if God's people will bring all their tithes and offerings into the storehouse, God will open the windows of heaven and pour out superabundant blessing. Yet others see the church's tragic compromise and alliance with the world—its standards and its methods—as the origin of her present wretched condition. They affirm that the church must divorce herself from the world and return to her true Lover and Lord. Yet again many consider that the departure of the church from the "sound doctrine" of Scripture is to a large extent responsible for her anemic condition. They aver that before there can be revival blessing, the church must embrace the doctrines of the Word of God in their pristine purity.

These, then, are the reasons being offered for the church's dormant and decadent condition: lack of unity, failure to evangelize, neglect of God's rights in tithes and offerings, friendship with the world, heterodoxy and apostasy. But are not these things properly results, not *reasons?* Are not they who advocate these things confusing consequences with causes? Are we being directed to that which is really the cause of our present barrenness or to that which is actually the consequence of our condition? No one acquainted with the literature of revival will deny that as God's people are revived there follow as a result the following: a true spirit of unity among believers; a greatly increased interest in world evangelization; church treasuries filled and overflowing; a separation from all that savors of the spirit of the world; a return to the doctrines and teachings of the Bible in their fullness.

Where, then, are we to look for the basic cause of the

church's present condition and lack of revival? Our text provides the answer. It is in the realm of prayer that the church has failed and is failing. It is the prayer life of the church that is at fault; she has forsaken the place of prevailing prayer. R. B. Jones, in his book on the Welsh revival of 1904, *Rent Heavens,* emphasized that "God seems to have so ordained that most, if not indeed all, of His activities in the moral and spiritual realms should be the responses of His heart and power to the prayers of His people."[1]

We are profoundly convinced, therefore, that there can be no prayer more fitting for God's people at this present time than this prayer of the prophet Isaiah. For as R. B. Jones has well said: "Revival is the exact answer to such a sigh as that of Isaiah 64:1: 'Oh that Thou wouldest rend the heavens.' "[2] Isaiah's plea sums up in itself all that is characteristic of the prayer that brings revival blessing.

CONTEXT OF PRAYER

Let us carefully note the *context* of this prayer pattern for revival blessing. Through the inspiration of the Spirit of God, Isaiah envisages the time when God's people are in captivity. He reflects upon the brief tenure of the promised land by his people: "The people of thy holiness have possessed it [their inheritance] but a little while" (63:18). He bemoans the fact that their adversaries have destroyed God's dwelling place, "Our adversaries have trodden down thy sanctuary" (63:18). He laments that their cities have been laid waste, "Thy holy cities are a wilderness, Zion is a wilderness, Jerusalem a desolation" (64:10).

But in addition to all this, the prophet sees the sin and iniquity that has brought these tragic conditions upon his people. In a spirit of true repentance, he identifies himself with his people and confesses their sin to God: "We have sinned: . . . We are all as an unclean thing, and all our righteousnesses are as filthy rags" (64:5-6). He sees, too, the prevailing spiritual condition of his people: "There is none that calleth upon thy name, that stirreth up himself to take hold of thee" (64:7).

This, then, is the revealing context of this prayer pattern: God's people are in a state of backsliding. As punishment for their departure from the living God, their enemies have been allowed to invade their land, destroy their cities, and carry a large number of the people into captivity. The prevailing conditions among the people now are prayerlessness and indifference to their state.

And what of our own day? Is not the contemporary scene precisely parallel to that of Isaiah's day? Has not the church forgotten and forsaken the living God? Is she not now in captivity? Are not her enemies making vast inroads into her territory, taking captive her people? In the midst of it all, are there not only a few who are "laying hold of God"? Let us face the fact: The church is not fulfilling her divine purpose in the world today. On crucial matters, her voice is silent. Through her departure from God, she has brought great shame upon herself and ridicule upon the name of God.

But, asks someone, do not these conditions actually militate against the idea of revival? Do not the prophetic Scriptures indicate that this is to be the state of things in the last days? We grant that the Saviour Himself said that "because iniquity shall abound, the love of many shall wax cold" (Mt 24:12). But this is not an argument *against revival*. Rather it is an argument *for* revival! He who will read the history of revivals will discover that invariably the conditions—which we have seen are true of our day—have been the very conditions in the midst of which revival has begun. James Burns, in his book, *Revivals: Their Laws and Leaders,* writes, "We find preceding each revival a time of spiritual deadness, when faith has waxed dim, when no great hopes cheer men's hearts, and when a dull and heavy lethargy has settled upon the spiritual life of man."[3]

But to be aware of the conditions is not enough. In Isaiah, we have a man who, informed of the state to which God's people would be reduced, immediately began to pray that God would visit them in power and glory and deliver them from the cruel hand of the enemy. He was not merely a spectator; he saw himself as part of the entire situation and went to God in prayer. It is never sufficient for a child of God only to realize the situation; he must accept his responsibility to pray that God will act and vindicate His name.

CONTENT OF PRAYER

What is the *content* of this prayer pattern for revival blessing? What does Isaiah ask for? What are the essential elements of the effectual fervent prayer of a righteous man?

Isaiah prays: "Oh that thou wouldest rend the heavens, that thou wouldest come down." That is the basic plea—that God will come down, that God will visit His people in their misery and bondage.

Does this language seem strange to some? Does someone, in zeal for exactness of spiritual terminology feel that this is not a proper plea for the believing heart? Let us illustrate. In 1959, Queen Elizabeth and her husband Prince Philip visited Canada. Queen Elizabeth is the sovereign of the British dominion. She is the ruler at all times. But at the request of her people and to open the great St. Lawrence Seaway, she visited Canada. In the same way, though God rules in the hearts of His people, though He is our gracious King and we His willing subjects, we invite Him in this prayer pattern to visit our hearts in a special way in all His majesty and royalty. That is revival: the King of heaven visiting His people in all His regal splendor and glory.

How we need just such a visitation today! Are our hearts barren, void of the fruits and flowers of the Spirit? Then we need the Lord to "come down like rain upon the mown grass: as showers that water the earth" (Ps 72:6). Are we in captivity, defeated and oppressed by our enemies? We need to pray the psalmist's prayer: "Bow thy heavens, O LORD, and come down: touch the mountains, and they shall smoke" (Ps 144:5).

Isaiah speaks of God's visitation under the figure of fire. He sees that when God visits His people, He comes as purifying flame: "The mountains flow down at His presence." This is what is meant by the price of revival. As J. D. Drysdale once wrote, "That there is a price to be paid for revival few who are familiar with the Scriptures and with revival literature will deny."[4]

When God visits His people, mountains of pride, bigotry, selfishness, indifference, and other sin, flow away; denominational, racial, and social barriers are broken down, all that hinders God's people from being one in Christ.

"Our God is a consuming fire." Are we prepared to pay the price? Are we ready for His gracious presence to be manifested in our midst? Are we willing to sing in sincerity and truth,

> Oh, that in me the sacred fire
> Might now begin to glow:
> Burn up the dross of base desire,
> And make the mountains flow!
>
> CHARLES WESLEY

Our age has a mania for results. Indeed everything is measured by the test, "Will it bring results?" It is not too much to say that in certain circles—professedly fundamental—the results now justify the means and methods used in the preaching of the gospel. But once we become concerned about God's presence in our midst, results will take care of themselves. Isaiah indicates that when God does visit His people as a purifying flame, there are sure and certain results: mountains flow down at His presence; adversaries are made to know His name; nations tremble at His presence.

We have here an individual action that in turn becomes international in its outreach. Like the ripples set in motion by a pebble thrown into a lake, this revival blessing starts with the individual and radiates to the ends of the earth. That is the kind of work that we need done today.

Isaiah reminds God that He has visited His people in just such a way in times past, "When thou didst terrible things which we looked not for, thou camest down, the mountains flowed down at thy presence." This is the reasoning of faith, "If God has visited his people before, He can and will do so again." Thus James McQuilkin, one of the human instruments in the Ulster Awakening in 1859, reasoned, after he had read *A Narrative of the Lord's Dealing with George Muller,* "Why may we not have such a blessed work here, seeing that God did such things for Mr. Muller simply in answer to prayer?"[5]

We have another example of faith's logic in Psalm 44:1, 4. The psalmist begins, "We have heard with our ears, O God, our fathers have told us, what work thou didst in their days, in the times of old." Then he proceeds to pray, "Thou art my King, O God: command deliverances for Jacob." May we, then, be greatly encouraged by what God has done in the past to ask Him to work again in our day.

CHARACTERISTICS OF PRAYER

Now let us see the *characteristics* of this prayer, for it is ever true, as Adam Clarke observed, that "a right prayer will have a ready answer."[6]

Isaiah prays in a spirit of true repentance. There must be a deep sorrow for sin and clear confession of it to God.

Isaiah is definite as he prays. He tells God what he wants Him to do on his behalf. This is a characteristic of all the prayers of the Bible. On the other hand, so much of our praying is vague and indefinite. And if we aim at nothing, we will be sure to hit it.

The soul may approach the Throne of grace assured that the golden scepter is extended toward it in favor. "Ask what I shall do for thee," is the invitation to all who feel their desperate need of blessing. We are to ask "in faith, nothing wavering. For he that wavereth is like a wave of the sea driven with the wind and tossed. For let not that man think that he shall receive anything of the Lord" (Ja 1:6-7).

As someone has well said, "Cold prayers never have warm answers." J. D. Drysdale wrote, "One of the sad evidences of the backslidden condition of the Church is that it has lost the 'Oh' from its prayers." [7] "If the arrow of prayer is to enter Heaven, we must draw it from a soul full bent," stated Bishop Hopkins. [8] It is "the effectual *fervent* prayer of a righteous man" that "availeth much" (Ja 5:16).

These then are the qualities, the characteristics of the prayer for revival blessing: repentance, definiteness, confidence, and fervency. Do our prayers possess these qualities? Only as they do will they "avail much" in the cause of revival.

We have sought to trace the cause of the church's present predicament. We have seen that it lies in the realm of prayer. We have learned that the church is truly in "captivity," defeated and oppressed. We have emphasized both the essential content and characteristics of the prayer for revival blessing. Let us all pray intelligently and insistently, frequently and fervently, until we see that revival blessing for which we seek.

LET US RETURN

Come, let us to the Lord our God
   With contrite hearts return;
Our God is gracious, nor will leave
   The desolate to mourn.

His voice commands the tempest forth,
   And stills the stormy wave;
And though His arm be strong to smite,
   'Tis also strong to save.

Long hath the night of sorrow reign'd;
   The dawn shall bring us light;
God shall appear, and we shall rise
   With gladness in His sight.

Our hearts, if God we seek to know,
   Shall know Him and rejoice;
His coming like the morn shall be,
   Like morning songs His voice.

As dew upon the tender herb,
   Diffusing fragrance round;
As showers that usher in the spring
   And cheer the thirsty ground.

So shall His presence bless our souls
   And shed a joyful light;
That hallow'd morn shall chase away
   The sorrows of the night.

JOHN MORRISON

6

THE PRELUDE TO REVIVAL

*Come, and let us return unto the Lord: for he
hath torn, and he will heal us; he hath smitten, and
he will bind us up. After two days he will revive
us: in the third day he will raise us up, and we
shall live in his sight. Then shall we know, if we
follow on to know the Lord: his going forth is prepared as the morning; and he shall come unto us as
the rain, as the latter and former rain unto the
earth.* HOSEA 6:1-3

HERE IS A PAGE from God's handbook on revival. It is not
concerned with regeneration; it majors on restoration. It is
not a prayer for life, but for abundant life. It has in view the
revival of God's people.

REVIVAL COLLECTIVELY DESIRED

In Hosea's response, the experience of revival is collectively desired. Read the paragraph again, noting the collective
aspects: "Come, and let *us* return unto the LORD: for he hath
torn, and he will heal *us;* he hath smitten, and he will bind *us*
up. After two days will he revive *us:* in the third day he will
raise *us* up, and *we* shall live in his sight. Then shall *we* know,
if *we* follow on to know the LORD: his going forth is prepared
as the morning; and he shall come unto *us* as the rain, as the
latter and former rain unto the earth."

As the church of Christ has become lukewarm, individual

Christians have contented themselves with a doctrine of personal revival; that is, we have told one another, amid the barrenness of the church, that general revival may not be possible but that we can at least know individual revival. While we do not dispute the necessity and possibility of such reviving, we suggest that one result of such a position is that as believers we have failed to desire revival collectively. In their homes, individual Christians may have been praying for revival, but there have been few church prayer meetings for revival.

In the words of Hosea 6:1-3, the prophet envisions the people of God as a whole, awakened to their need, encouraging one another to return to the Lord.

It is difficult perhaps to separate this collective desire for revival from revival itself. Is such prayer the prelude to revival or the first phase of revival? We may not be able to make such fine distinctions and definitions, but surely such desire for the blessing of revival brings a group of God's people to the border of their promised land.

NEED CLEARLY DEMONSTRATED

In Hosea's words the need for revival *is clearly demonstrated.* "Come, and let us return unto the Lord: for he hath torn, and he will heal us; he hath smitten, and he will bind us up." The condition of God's people is given in the two words *torn* and *smitten.* What is meant by these words?

Because of the chapter division, it is easy to lose sight of the context of Hosea 6:1-3. In Hosea 5:14, however, we have the explanation of the condition of God's people. There the Lord says, "I will be unto Ephraim as a lion, and as a young lion to the house of Judah: I, even I, will tear and go away; I will take away, and none shall rescue him."

When, therefore, God's people describe themselves as torn and smitten, they are referring to the results of God's judgment upon them. Earlier they had been chastised by God, and that judgment resulted in their being torn and smitten, wounded and bleeding.

Historically, in the case of Israel, this was fulfilled in the attack of the Assyrian army. The Assyrians entered the land and defeated Israel. It is most important to notice that when the people of God consider that judgment they trace it not to the hand of the Assyrian but to the hand of God. It was God, acting like a roaring, ravenous lion, who judged their land. He was sovereign in the nature and results of the judgment.

Here is an aspect of the church's present plight and predicament that may have been overlooked. God has sovereignly allowed His people to go their own way and to learn the fearful consequences of departing from God. God's judgments have in view the ultimate repentance of His people. "I will go and return to my place," affirms the Lord, "till they acknowledge their offense, and seek my face: in their affliction they will seek me early" (5:15).

In the case of Israel, the Lord could easily have held back the Assyrian invader; that He did not is evidence that He was employing the enemy as His own scourge. That God could defeat the forces of materialism and humanism that have assaulted the church is also clear; that God has allowed the church to be ravaged by these adversaries is evidence that He is displeased with His people and is disciplining them for their sins. We, too, have been torn and smitten.

There is an interesting and informative statement made about Israel in Hosea 5:13. "When Ephraim saw his sickness, and Judah saw his wound, then went Ephraim to the Assyrian, and sent to king Jareb: yet could he not heal you, nor cure you of your wound." This verse tells us that Israel did not return immediately to the Lord. First, the help of the Assyrian was sought. How bitter for Israel to find out later that the Assyrian was no friend but really a foe, and that the Assyrian was to be the instrument of their scourging!

69

And what has the church done in her affliction? Have we not been seeking the help of all kinds of quack doctors, hoping that relief and recovery will come through their ministrations? Have we not looked to man for help and hope rather than to God? The church in North America is presently looking toward a social gospel as the answer to its problems. We have yet to learn that such a gospel cannot heal us or cure us of our wounds.

NATURE CAREFULLY DEFINED

What, then, is the nature of revival? In Hosea's words the nature of revival is carefully defined. "Come, and let us return unto the LORD: for he hath torn, and he will heal us; he hath smitten, and he will bind us up. After two days will he revive us: in the third day he will raise us up."

Revival is the healing of God's people. It is the binding up of their wounds. It is being raised up from the sickbed. It is to receive health and strength, not primarily in a physical sense, but in the spiritual. Revival is "the recovery of spiritual health. It is the church's spring time. It is the jubilee of holiness. It is the feast of fat things. It is the beauty of the Lord."[1]

God is not only the Parent who chastises His children; He is the Physician who heals them. How wise and skillful He is in His ministry of healing!

What does the prophet mean by the words of Hosea 6:2, "After two days will he revive us: in the third day will he raise us up"? Many commentators have seen in this statement a prophecy of the resurrection of Christ; that is, the passage has been made Messianic in character.

We would suggest, however, that what is being spoken of is the speedy recovery of God's people. Remember that they have been mauled by a lion (Ho 5:14). Their condition is desperate. They have been torn and smitten. But now in returning to the Lord, they find restoration and health are miraculously provided. "After two days will he revive us:

70

in the third day he will raise us up." Think of it—a patient whose condition is desperate is up and walking in three short days! Just as speedy is true revival. Sin-sick souls are touched by the great Physician and are restored to spiritual vigor.

CONSEQUENCE CONCISELY DESCRIBED

But note that in Hosea's words, the consequence of revival is concisely described. "Come, and let us return unto the LORD: . . . and we shall live in his sight" (6:1-2).

"We shall live in his sight." That is the consequence of true revival. Where formerly the church has been diseased and dying, when all the efforts of God's people have failed to resuscitate the fainting and feeble church; there and then when God intervenes, the church begins to live in power. It is not simply, "We shall live," but, "We shall live in his sight." Henceforth, all of life is lived consciously under the scrutiny of God. All matters are referred to Him for guidance and decision. From Him comes the sustenance for living and the goal of living.

Have you been seeking to live your life independently of God? You profess to be a Christian, but do your daily activities fail to be related consciously and continually to God? Revival will bring you into the place where you live your life in the sight of the Lord. Every responsibility and every relationship will be transfigured by such a consciousness. You will begin to know the approval of God upon your life and witness.

How desperately this kind of revival is needed among us! We do not need more posters, programs, or parades. We need more specific prayer for God's intervention in our desperate situation. We need to be touched so that we shall live in His sight.

To live in the sight of the Lord is to live seeking His favor and approval. It involves walking in the fear of the Lord, manifesting godliness and holiness of life.

But there is a further truth to be derived from Hosea's response to God. In his words the certainty of revival is confidently declared.

"Let us return unto the LORD," appeals the prophet, "after two days will he revive us." If we *return,* He will *revive.*

Does this appear to be too mechanical? Is this daring to offer a formula for revival that makes the steps to spiritual awakening too rigid? But what does God ask? In the same book from which our text is taken we read, "O Israel, return unto the LORD thy God; for thou hast fallen by thine iniquity. Take with you words, and turn to the LORD" (Ho 14:1-2). There is the same emphasis again. "Return."

This road to revival can be confirmed by a dozen texts. When we are prepared to humble ourselves and acknowledge that we have sinned, then we become candidates for God's reviving. "I will go," declares the Lord, "and return to my place, till they acknowledge their offense, and seek my face: in their affliction they will seek me early" (Ho 5:15). God withdraws and waits until His people admit their sin and submit to His authority.

The certainty of revival, then, when God's people return to the Lord, is based upon the revealed character of God. He withdraws His loving presence from His people, but only until they humble themselves and seek His face. Then He returns to bless and to save them from their predicament.

BLESSINGS COMPREHENSIVELY DEVELOPED

We note, finally, that in Hosea's words the *blessings of revival are comprehensively developed.* What an amazing verse is Hosea 6:3! How much truth is compressed into it! Here it is from the *New American Standard Bible:* "So let us know, let us press on to know the LORD. His going forth is as certain as the dawn; And He will come to us like the rain, like the spring rain watering the earth."

The blessings of revival include a relationship to be enjoyed. We are encouraged to "press on to know the Lord" in intimate fellowship and communion. The prophet is not calling for us to know more about God merely from a theoretical viewpoint. He is speaking of a living, dynamic, transforming relationship. "Revival," affirms Norman Grubb, "is really the Reviver in action."[2]

It was because this kind of knowledge of God was missing from their lives that the people of Israel were judged. Indeed, the concept of knowledge is one of the key ideas of the prophecy of Hosea. In Hosea 4:1, for example, the prophet laments that "there is no truth, nor mercy, nor knowledge of God in the land." In the same chapter he affirms: "My people are destroyed for lack of knowledge" (4:6). In chapter 5 verse 4, the charge is levelled against the people that "they have not known the LORD."

This is precisely the great lack in our churches today. People are not enjoying a personal relationship with God. They know little or nothing about day-by-day communion with Him through His Word and in prayer. It is not that these aspects have been stressed in today's churches; they have been repeatedly! The problem lies deeper. People have not entered into that relationship, and they have not enjoyed that experience.

But the blessings of revival include a sunrise to be experienced. "His going forth," proclaims the prophet, "is as certain as the dawn." The period before revival may be best described as a time of gloom and darkness. Saints fall asleep, and little is done in God's vineyard. Revival, on the other hand, can be described as a sunrise. The Sun of righteousness rises with healing in His wings (Mal 4:2). The blessed Saviour dispels the darkness of our night and shines upon us in His brightness and glory.

73

The blessings of revival also include a refreshing to be received. "He will come to us like the rain, like the spring rain watering the earth." The sad condition of drought and barrenness is to be transformed by the showers of blessing from the presence of the Lord.

Perhaps no verse summarizes what the Lord means to His people in revival as much as 2 Samuel 23:4, "He shall be as the light of the morning, when the sun riseth, even a morning without clouds; as the tender grass springing out of the earth by clear shining after rain."

Is revival with all of its attendant and subsequent blessings possible in our time? Thank God, it is when we repent and return to the Lord. "After two days will he revive us: in the third day he will raise us up, and we shall live in his sight."

CHRIST'S GREAT GIFT

When the Saviour rose to glory,
There to share His Father's throne,
Leaving here, to tell His story,
All His chosen and His own.
As a parting pledge of favour
His most precious gift He sent,
Even the Eternal Spirit—
Crown of Christ's new covenant.

A Convictor to accuse us,
To rebuke the pride within;
With the two-edged sword to smite us
And expose our hidden sin.
Then a Comforter to cheer us,
To remind us of the Blood,
Bringing rest to troubled conscience,
Showing we have peace with God.

Christ, we come for living water,
That the desert lands around
Also may be rich and fertile
And with fruits of love abound.

Fiery Spirit, Wind from Heaven,
Oh, we need revival now!
Stir us, rouse us from our slumber,
With full strength and pow'r endow.
May each member of Christ's body
Exercise his special gift,
That together to all nations
We the Cross may soon uplift.

ALEX V. WILSON
Used by permission

7

THE PURPOSE OF REVIVAL

Wilt thou not revive us again: that thy people may rejoice in thee?" PSALM 85:6

FEW PASSAGES of God's Word correct our misconceptions of revival as does Psalm 85, the key verse of which is verse 6, "Wilt thou not revive us again: that thy people may rejoice in thee?" All our ideas about revival must be tested by the criteria of Scripture, not by reason or by experience.

THE TRUE APPLICANT FOR REVIVAL

We begin by noticing that this verse, along with the entire psalm, clarifies our thinking with regard to the true applicant for revival. "Wilt thou not revive us again: that thy people may rejoice in thee?" Who is here voicing a heart cry for revival? Who is speaking in these words?

Well, it is certainly not the world at large. No cry ever comes from the hearts of the unsaved for spiritual revival and renewal. In the very nature of things, the unsaved world knows nothing about being revived. All is death, both moral and spiritual, in the hearts of those without God and without Christ. What the unsaved need is regeneration, not revival. Indeed, speak of revival to the typical man of this age, and he will wonder what you are talking about. Explain it to him, and he will either laugh at you or try to explain away the whole phenomenon on the basis of psychological theory. It is emphatically not the world at large that is crying out for revival.

Again, this passionate prayer for revival is not the plea of the carnal believer, the one who is cold and calloused toward the divine working. This prayer is not voiced by those who belong to that group described by Isaiah the prophet, "There is none that calleth upon thy name, that stirreth up himself to take hold of thee" (Is 64:7). This cry for divine intervention comes not from the hearts of those who are lukewarm or disinterested.

Who, then, offers this prayer to God? It is the prayer of a minority of God's people who have been awakened and aroused to a consciousness of their need and who are applying to heaven for immediate relief.

A study of Psalm 85 in its entirety reveals the characteristics of these people who are the true applicants for revival.

Look, for example, at verses 1-3. The psalmist prays: "LORD, thou hast been favourable unto thy land: Thou hast brought back the captivity of Jacob. Thou hast forgiven the iniquity of thy people, thou hast covered all their sin. Selah. Thou hast taken away all thy wrath: Thou hast turned thyself from the fierceness of thine anger."

Regardless of the way in which we interpret these verses (either as an account of some past deliverance of God's people or an anticipation of some future deliverance of Israel), they tell us much about the people who crave God's intervention.

First, they are a people who are conscious of the dominion of sin. "Thou hast brought back the captivity of Jacob." Sin leads to bondage. It rules with an iron hand.

That, tragically, is the condition of many of God's people today. They are the victims of materialism and selfishness. They are under the dominion of sin and know not the way to freedom. They desperately need to be delivered from their captivity.

But we learn that the true applicants for revival are those who are conscious of the defilement of sin. Sin not only binds; it blackens. It captivates, and it contaminates the soul. When God delivers the soul, therefore, He also deals with the sin of the soul. "Thou hast covered all their sin."

Finally, we learn that the true applicants for revival are those who are conscious of the distress of sin. Sin not only binds and darkens the soul, it also brings the soul under the righteous judgment of God. Thus, anticipating God's deliverance by faith, the psalmist is able to affirm, "Thou hast taken away all thy wrath: Thou hast turned thyself from the fierceness of thy wrath."

But for the present he prays, "Turn us, O God of our salvation, and cause thine anger toward us to cease. Wilt thou be angry with us forever? wilt thou draw out thine anger to all generations?" (85:4-5).

Is not this a strand of biblical teaching that the church has lost sight of in our day? Is not God angry with a sinful, lukewarm, and complacent church? Let us not try to convince ourselves by any application (or misapplication) of dispensational teaching that God is indifferent to the sins of His people today. We recognize that in Psalm 85 it is the nation of Israel that is primarily represented, but we are not thereby prepared to say that there is no application of the principles set forth in this psalm to the church today. We do not claim that the church has replaced Israel, but we do suggest that the church's experience is reflected in Israel's history.

These, then, are the people who are the true applicants for revival. They are living in the church's wintertime, when everything around is frozen over with ice and snow; but they are looking for the church's springtime. They are living in the valley of dry bones, but they are pleading, like Ezekiel, for the Spirit of life to come, who will quicken the dry bones into life.

"Wilt thou not revive us again: that thy people may rejoice in thee?" This verse clarifies our thinking with regard to the true applicant for revival: it also helps us to understand the true antecedent of revival. We speak now of prayer itself. The first part of the psalm itself is in the form of a prayer. It is addressed directly to the Lord. The psalmist is approaching the mercy seat with his plea. He is crying to God for the reviving of His people. Like Queen Esther, he is coming to the throne of grace on behalf of a desperately needy people.

The true antecedent of revival is not costly publicity, charismatic personalities, or carnal pressure. It is when God's people pray that revival comes.

This claim may be amply established from the study of past revivals. Prayer for revival has always preceded the awakening of God's people.

Recall some prayers from the Bible:

It was after Elijah had prayed on Mount Carmel that the fire of the Lord fell.

It was after Ezekiel had prayed for the breath of heaven in the valley of dry bones that the skeletons came together and came to life.

It was after Samuel had prayed to the Lord at Mizpeh that Israel defeated her enemies.

It was after the disciples had prayed in the upper room that the Spirit of God filled each waiting heart.

We could add testimony after testimony showing that every true revival, every lasting revival, every fruitful revival, has had as its antecedent believing, faith-filled, fervent prayer.

But listen to the testimony of various men of God, greatly used in revival since Bible times.

G. W. Hervey, whose handbook on revivals is a classic,

wrote, "The foremost means of getting ready for a general awakening is prayer."[1]

C. G. Finney, whose ministry as a man of God, mightily used in revival, is well known, stated, "Prayer produces such a change in us and fulfills such conditions as renders it consistent for God to do as it would not be consistent for Him to do otherwise."[2]

W. B. Pearce wrote, "Prayer is the starting point of revival."[3]

C. E. Autrey claimed that "prayer is one feature which is found in every great revival."[4]

Theodore Bamber asserted, "Revival is inaugurated by prayer only."[5]

Many illustrations could be provided of this great principle that prayer precedes every genuine revival of God's people. Let us share one from the life of DeWitt Talmage, American pastor and preacher.

On one occasion Dr. Talmage, oppressed beyond measure by the fact that conversions were not more numerous, invited to his house five Christian men. These men came, not knowing why they had been invited.

"I took them," said Talmage, "to the top room of my house. I said to them: 'I have called you here for special prayer. I am in an agony for a great turning to God of the people. Let us kneel down in prayer, and not leave this room until we are all assured that the blessing will come, and has come.'

"It was a most intense crying to God. I said to them, 'Let this meeting be a secret.' And they said it would be.

"On the following Friday night occurred the usual prayer meeting. No one knew what had taken place on the former occasion, but the meeting was unusually thronged. Men accustomed to pray in great composure broke down under deep emotion; the people were in tears. There were sobs and silences and solemnities of such unusual power that the wor-

81

shippers looked into each other's faces as much as to say, 'What does all this mean?'

"When the following Sunday came, over four hundred rose for prayer, and a religious awakening took place which made that winter memorable for time and eternity."[6]

We should read Psalm 85 again to discover just what kind of prayer it is that precedes revival. It is not the general type of prayer to which we are accustomed. It is not composed of pious platitudes and high-sounding generalities.

It is the prayer which is marked by the confession of sin. The psalmist speaks of the iniquity and the sin of his people.

It is the prayer which is marked by the concept of God as a God of holiness and righteousness.

It is the prayer which is marked by the contemplation of the work of Christ on the cross. "Mercy and truth are met together; righteousness and peace have kissed each other" (85:10).

THE TRUE AUTHOR OF REVIVAL

"Wilt thou not revive us again: that thy people may rejoice in thee?" How this verse helps us to understand the true applicant for revival and the true antecedent of revival! It also helps us to understand the true Author of revival. "Wilt thou"—there is the emphasis. It is Jehovah (85:1), the God of our salvation (85:4), God the Lord (85:8), who is the Author of revival. David Matthews summarized the truth well: "Divine movements have their birthplace in the heart of Deity."[7] Alexander Whyte, who himself had witnessed revival in the north of Scotland, wrote, "There is a divine mystery about revivals. God's sovereignty is in them."[8]

Having affirmed this truth, however, we must say that often our understanding of a truth can be marred by a false emphasis or extreme. In emphasizing that God alone can grant or give revival to His people, we must guard against any tendency or teaching that would relieve us of our responsibility in the matter of revival. Duncan Campbell, a man who saw genuine revival in the Hebrides, warned, "God is the God of revival. He is sovereign in the affairs of men. . . . But we must not believe in any conception of God's sovereignty that nullifies man's responsibility."[9]

A few cautions, therefore, may be helpful at this point.

In affirming that God is sovereign in revival, we must not thereby conclude that it is not necessary to preach the Word of God.

In stressing that it is God who grants revival, we must not imagine that there is no need of our assembling together and seeking God's face.

In pointing out that God awakens His people, we must not become complacent and slumber on in our indifference. We must stir ourselves.

In teaching that God is the true Author of revival, we are not, therefore, concluding that there is no need for a continual heart examination before Him.

What, then, is the balance of truth in this whole matter? We must preach, pray, meet together, work, witness, and live with a clear recognition that these things in themselves cannot produce revival, but that they are the appointed means of securing such a revival in the allwise and sovereign plan of God.

THE TRUE AIM OF REVIVAL

"Wilt thou not revive us again: that thy people may rejoice in thee?" This simple text clarifies our thinking in the areas of the true applicant for revival, the true antecedent of revival, and the true Author of revival. But it also guides us in our thinking about the true aim of revival.

The psalmist is explicit: "That thy people may rejoice in thee." The aim of revival, therefore, is not primarily the deliverance of the church from her wretched plight. It is not the transformation of our society. It is not the solving of our problems—whether personal, ecclesiastical, or national. It is, rather, that God's people may rejoice in God Himself.

There can be no more solemn or serious questions for the believer to ask himself than, What is the source of my present joy? In what do I delight constantly and continually? In whom do I rejoice?

The Scriptures reveal that the revived heart rejoices in God. Let us amplify that for a moment.

The revived heart rejoices in the salvation of God: "I will rejoice in thy salvation" (Ps 9:14).

The revived heart rejoices in the sovereignty of God: "The Lord reigneth; let the earth rejoice" (Ps 97:1).

The revived heart rejoices in the Word of God: "I rejoice at thy Word, as one that findeth great spoil" (Ps 119:162).

The revived heart rejoices in the protection of God: "Because thou hast been my help, therefore in the shadow of thy wings will I rejoice" (Ps 63:7).

The revived heart rejoices in the justice of God: "The righteous shall see it [the providential just dealings of God] and rejoice" (Ps 107:42).

The revived heart rejoices in the name of God: "In thy name shall they rejoice all the day" (Ps 89:16).

The revived heart rejoices in God Himself: "Rejoice in the Lord, O ye righteous" (Ps 33:1).

"Wilt thou not revive us again: that thy people may rejoice in thee?" As we have studied this prayer for revival, we have seen how it corrects our thinking with regard to the true applicant for revival, the true antecedent of revival, the true Author of revival, and the true aim of revival. But the question may arise, Was this prayer for revival answered? If Psalm 85 was written before the exile of Israel or during the exile of Israel, then it is most instructive to set Psalm 85:6

side by side with Ezra 9:8-9, which, of course, was written after the exile.

Here are the two passages placed together: "Wilt thou not revive us again: that thy people may rejoice in thee?" (Ps 85:6) "Now for a little space grace hath been shewed from the Lord our God, . . . that our God may lighten our eyes, and give us a little reviving in our bondage. For we were bondmen; yet our God hath not forsaken us in our bondage, but hath extended mercy unto us in the sight of the kings of Persia, to give us a reviving" (Ezra 9:8-9)

Does not the Ezra passage complement Psalm 85:6? The psalmist prayed for a reviving of God's people; Ezra saw in Israel's return from the Babylonian exile at least a partial answer to the psalmist's prayer. God revived His people by bringing them back into the land of their inheritance.

How, then, shall we employ the words of Psalm 85:6 for our own needs today? Harold P. Barker tells of one David Dodge in conversation with a devout Quaker who, like Dodge, was eager to see a revival. The Quaker agreed with Dodge concerning the need of more enthusiasm, more prayer, more consecration. Finally the Quaker broke in with, "Friend Dodge, suppose thee and I make a beginning!"[10]

That's it! Suppose "thee and I" make a beginning. Remember that *I* is central to the word *revival!*

GIVE ME THINE HEART

Lord, when my heart was whole, I kept it back
  And grudged to give it Thee.
Now when that it is broken, must I lack
  Thy kind word, "Give it Me"?
Silence would be but just, and Thou art just.
Yet since I lie here shattered in the dust,
  With still an eye to lift to Thee,
A broken heart to give,
I think that Thou wilt bid me live,
  And answer, "Give it Me."

C. G. ROSSETTI

I'll give my heart to Jesus,
  'Tis all the gift He'll prize;
A broken and a contrite heart
  I'm sure He'll not despise.

I'll give my heart to Jesus,
  I've nothing else to give
That would be worthy to bestow,
  Or Jesus would receive.

I've nothing else to give Him;
  No gold, nor gems of worth,
And what would these be unto Him,
  The Lord of all the earth?

Oh, take my heart, dear Saviour,
  And make it wholly Thine,
That 'mid the jewels in Thy crown
  Forever it may shine.

JOSEPHINE POLLARD

8

THE PRICE OF REVIVAL

*For thus saith the high and lofty One that in-
habiteth eternity, whose name is Holy; I dwell in
the high and holy place, with him also that is of a
contrite and humble spirit, to revive the spirit of
the humble, and to revive the heart of the contrite
ones.* ISAIAH 57:15

WHY DOES REVIVAL TARRY? If, as Norman Grubb claims,
brokenness is the key word in continuous revival,[1] then we
need look no further to explain the lack of genuine revival in
the Christian church today. Brokenness is an aspect of Christian experience that is sadly and seriously neglected in the
current emphasis upon spiritual renewal. "By their fruits ye
shall know them" is a valid test we may apply to every message or movement claiming the church's attention. And by
this test much of the emphasis upon new life in the church
is found wanting. Of many preachers and teachers, we must
confess there is brilliance but there is no brokenness.

In the Old Testament, various words are used for this concept of being broken, each with its distinctive shade of meaning. The word that is used to describe a broken heart may
also be translated "shattered." It is so used in Jeremiah 2:13
in the graphic phrase "broken cisterns, that can hold no
water." It is used in Ezekiel 27:34 to describe the breaking up of a great and noble ship in the midst of a storm. It
is used in Ezekiel 34:4 to describe a sheep that has fallen

from a height and has suffered broken bones. And it is used in Daniel 8:22 to describe the rough goat's horn that was broken off by its adversary.

These word pictures serve to emphasize the basic idea, namely, of being shattered, of being entirely broken to pieces. Thus, when the authors of the Bible use the word to describe a human heart, they refer to a heart that through some devastating experience has been shattered to pieces. What formerly was whole and hard and adamant has been utterly broken and fragmented and pulverized. Brokenness, therefore, is that frame and attitude of heart in which the individual takes his place before God in lowliness, confessing his need of divine grace and assistance.

Brokenness is the soul, like the shattered cistern, empty of its own confidence and resources.

Brokenness is the soul, like the ship, shipwrecked on God.

Brokenness is the soul, like the sheep, broken through its own foolish wanderings and lying at the feet of the merciful Shepherd of souls.

Brokenness is the soul, like the animal of Daniel's vision, bereft of its former power and might, now submissive before the almighty God.

We should note that the term brokenhearted or broken in heart does not occur frequently in Scripture. However, although the term itself does not appear often, the concept is represented by other basic words, such as contrite, humble, and poor.

That we may come to grips directly with our subject, let us ask—and answer—four basic questions:

First, how is brokenness to be *regarded* by us?

Second, how is brokenness to be *recognized* with regard to its essential features?

Third, how is brokenness to be *realized* and manifested in the church?

Fourth, how is brokenness to be *retained* and preserved?

First, then, let us determine how brokenness is to be regarded by us who profess to be disciples of the meek and lowly Jesus. Consider the following selected Scriptures:

Psalm 34:18—"The Lord is nigh unto them that are of a broken heart; and saveth such as be of a contrite spirit." Here brokenness is regarded as the essential condition for God's presence in saving power. The Lord hastens to the rescue of the brokenhearted.

Psalm 51:17—"The sacrifices of God are a broken spirit: a broken and a contrite heart, O God, thou wilt not despise." According to this writer, brokenness is to be regarded as the one essential condition for God's acceptance and favor. The psalmist realized that God takes no delight in burnt offerings that are not accompanied by broken hearts.

Isaiah 66:2—"To this man will I look, even to him that is poor and of a contrite spirit, and trembleth at my word." Again, brokenness is made the one essential condition for God's special favor and blessing. God "looks" in the direction of the man with a broken heart.

Isaiah 57:15—"I dwell in the high and holy place, with him also that is of a contrite and humble spirit, to revive the spirit of the humble, and to revive the heart of the contrite ones." This is *the* text that teaches brokenness as a key word of revival. God's presence is not made manifest in a person whose heart is not broken before Him.

Isaiah 61:1—"The Spirit of the Lord God is upon me; because the Lord hath anointed me to preach good tidings unto the meek; he hath sent me to bind up the brokenhearted." God sends not an angel, not an archangel, but His Son to bind up the broken in heart. Thus brokenness is made the one essential condition for God's visitation in the person of His Son.

There can be no doubt, then, that from a scriptural standpoint, brokenness is to be regarded by us as the one essential condition of heart for God's response to us in our need, whatever that need may be. If we are to be blessed by God, He has required that we come before Him with broken hearts and contrite spirits.

How should we regard brokenness of heart? Let the question put to a missionary working in Africa among Christians who had known times of gracious revival provide the answer. Whenever the missionary mentioned the name of any Christian, the African Christians would ask, "But is he a broken Christian?"[2] Surely the seventeenth-century writer, George Cokeyn, was right when he wrote, "Brokenness is that which God doth principally and more especially look after in all our approaches and accesses to Him."[3]

How Is Brokenness to Be Recognized?

Our second question leads us deeper into our discussion. How is brokenness to be recognized? What are the characteristics of contriteness, the marks of brokenness?

First, a brokenhearted person is deeply conscious of the majesty of God. The brokenhearted person has seen the Lord God, high and lifted up on His throne of splendour and strength. The attributes of God—His holiness, His power, His sovereignty—become impressively vital and vivid; no longer are they dry doctrines in a theology textbook, but living facts that awaken a sense of awe and adoration in the contrite heart.

Do we have this consciousness, this conviction of the majesty of our God? Or do we talk glibly about Him, making reference to Him in the cheap and vulgar language of the day as "the Man up in the sky," far removed from His creation and unconcerned about His creatures? Brokenness of heart shows itself first in an awareness of the greatness and glory of the God with whom we have to do.

But, second, a brokenhearted person is deeply conscious of

the meaning of sin. This follows, of course, as a direct result of the first aspect. Let us once see God truly, and we will see ourselves. Isaiah saw the Lord, and that vision brought an exposure of the prophet himself. Peter saw the Lord Jesus on the shore of the Sea of Galilee, and seeing Him in His majesty, he begged Him to leave, saying, "I am a sinful man, O Lord" (Lk 5:8).

In his book *Revivals: Their Laws and Leaders,* James Burns states that as a general principle, every revival sees an awakening of a deep sense of sin in the individual and in the church. "In the intense spiritual light, the sin and guilt of the awakened soul stand out in terrifying blackness."[4]

Third, a brokenhearted person is deeply conscious of the mercy of God in Christ. You may stand in Eden and become conscious of the heinousness of human sin; you may stand at Sinai and catch something of the majesty of God; but it is when you come to Calvary and there gaze on the Son of God suffering on account of your sin that your heart will be broken. It is as the heart is overwhelmed by a consciousness that God in Christ is gracious and merciful to the sinner that it breaks down in tears and anguish.

How Is Brokenness to Be Realized?

We have considered how brokenness is to be regarded by us—as the essential heart condition as we come before God. We have considered how brokenness is to be recognized—by an awareness of the majesty of God, the meaning of sin, and the mercy of God in Christ. Let us seek now to learn how brokenness is to be realized in our experience, that is, how it is to be achieved.

Generally, we may say that the human heart is broken by the Word of God applied by the Spirit of God to us at the point of our deepest need. The human heart may be looked upon as the adamant stone, the Word of God as the hammer, and the Holy Spirit the one who wields the hammer to break up the hard, unyielding stone. It is this aspect of the Word of God that is ever foremost when the heart is in the process of being broken—the Word is the Sword of the Spirit, rebuking, searching, piercing, and probing.

Perhaps the testimony of the Rev. A. Douglas Brown, a minister of the gospel who lived in the early part of this century, will throw more light upon this aspect of our subject than further explanation and exposition. Mr. Brown wrote the following, concerning his experience in his book *Revival Addresses*.

> I had been a minister of Jesus Christ for twenty-six years; then God laid hold of me in the midst of a Sunday evening service, and He nearly broke my heart while I was preaching. I went back to the vestry and locked the door, and threw myself down on the hearthrug in front of the vestry fireplace, brokenhearted. Why? I do not know.
>
> My church was filled. I loved my people, and I believe my people loved me. I do not say they ought to, but they did. I was as happy there as I could be. I had never known a Sunday there for fifteen years without conversions. If you do not have conversions in your church, it does not matter what the name of it is, that church has a name to live, but is dead.
>
> That night I went home and went straight up to my study. My wife came to tell me that supper was ready, and was waiting. "You must not wait supper for me," I said.
>
> "What is the matter?" she asked.
>
> "I have a broken heart," I replied.
>
> It was worth while having a broken heart for Jesus to mend it. I had no supper that night. Christ laid His hand on a proud minister, and told him that he had not gone far enough, that there were reservations in his surrender, and He wanted him to do a piece of work that he had been trying to evade. I knew what He meant.
>
> All November that struggle went on, but I would not give way; I knew God was right, and I knew I was wrong. I knew what it would mean for me, and I was not prepared to pay the price. Then Christmas time came, and all the joy round

about seemed to mock me. I knew what Jesus wanted. He showed me pictures of congregations, and Douglas Brown on his knees in the midst of them.

I saw Douglas Brown praying with his own folk, to whom he had preached for over fifteen years. I saw it all in picture.

The struggle went on, and I said to the Lord, "You know, that is not my work. I will pray for anyone else who does it, but please do not give it to me; it will kill me. I cannot get up into the pulpit and plead with people. It is against my temperament, and You made me."

All through January, God wrestled with me. There is a Love that will not let us go. Glory be to God! At the end of January, I was still like poor Jacob, struggling instead of clinging. I thought that what was wrong was my circumstances, when what was really wrong was Douglas Brown. We always put it down to our circumstances as long as we can.

It was in February, 1921, after four months of struggle, that there came the crisis. Oh, how patient God is! On the Saturday night I wrote out my resignation to my church, and it was marked with my own tears. I loved the church, but I felt that if I could not be holy I would be honest; I felt that I could not go on preaching while I had a contention with God. Whoever else you dupe, do not dupe God. If you grieve the Holy Ghost, the whole thing is done. That night the resignation lay on my blotter, and I went to bed, but not to sleep.

As I went out of the bedroom door the next morning, I stumbled over my dog. If ever I thanked God for my dog I did that night. As I knelt at my study table, the dog licked his master's face; he thought I was ill. When "Mike" was doing that, I felt that I did not deserve anybody to love me; I felt an outcast.

Then something happened. I found myself in the loving embrace of Christ for ever and ever; and all power and all joy and all blessedness rolled in like a deluge.[5]

How Is Brokenness to Be Retained?

Our final consideration raises the question: How may brokenness be retained? John Bunyan instructs us, "Even as

93

to *have* a broken heart is an excellent thing, so to *keep* a broken heart is an excellent thing."[6]

Once our hearts have been softened like wax in the sun, we must seek to keep them soft and pliable.

Once our hearts have been broken up by the plowshare of repentance, we must keep them in such a condition that the good seed of the Word of God may take root and bear fruit in our lives.

Once our hearts have been melted like ice placed near a fire, we must desire to keep them in that state. Is not this the meaning of Hannah's words when she spoke of her soul being poured out before the Lord? (1 Sa 1:15)

Negatively, some cautions may be given to the soul anxious to remain broken before the Lord.

Do not evade the Word of God as it comes to you in your need. When God speaks through His Word to your heart, then respond immediately. Don't hesitate to obey. Don't procrastinate.

Do not excuse known sin on any ground. Call sin by its right name. Deal with it definitely and drastically. It is the cold breath of sin that freezes the once-melted heart. Keep in the ray of the Sun of righteousness.

Do not entertain hard thoughts against God. Beware of unbelief. Nothing hardens the heart as quickly as unbelief.

Positively, some counsels may be given to the soul anxious to remain broken before the Lord.

Dwell much in the Word of God. God is known to us through His Word. It is the Word that gives instruction and enlightenment and correction.

Make much of the work of Christ on your behalf. Meditate much on the blood which was shed for you. Think much of His present ministry of intercession in heaven for you.

Ask much for the ministry of the Holy Spirit in your life. He is the Spirit of the glorified Jesus, the one who ascended to the Father's right hand.

SEND THE FIRE

Thou Christ of burning, cleansing flame,
   Send the fire!
Thy Blood-bought gift today we claim,
   Send the fire!
Look down and see this waiting host,
Give us the promised Holy Ghost,
We want another Pentecost,
   Send the fire!

God of Elijah, hear our cry!
   Send the fire!
Oh, make us fit to live or die,
   Send the fire!
To burn up every trace of sin,
To bring the light and glory in,
The revolution now begin,
   Send the fire!

'Tis fire we want, for fire we plead,
   Send the fire!
The fire will meet our ev'ry need,
   Send the fire!
For daily strength to do the right,
For grace to conquer in the fight,
For power to walk the world in white,
   Send the fire!

To make our weak hearts strong and brave,
   Send the fire!
To live a dying world to save;
   Send the fire!
Oh, see us on Thy altar lay
Our lives, our all, this very day;
To crown the off'ring now, we pray,
   Send the fire.

GENERAL WILLIAM BOOTH

9

THE POWER OF REVIVAL

And it came to pass at the time of the offering of the evening sacrifice, that Elijah the prophet came near, and said, Lord God of Abraham, Isaac, and of Israel, let it be known this day that thou art God in Israel, and that I am thy servant, and that I have done all these things at thy word.

Hear me, O Lord, hear me, that this people may know that thou art the Lord God, and that thou hast turned their heart back again.

Then the fire of the Lord fell, and consumed the burnt sacrifice, and the wood, and the stones, and the dust, and licked up the water that was in the trench. 1 KINGS 18:36-38

"THE FIRE OF THE LORD." These words, when lifted out of their context, suggest different things to different people.

To some, satisfied with the "no fire" of formalism, these words appear on the page like a red flag, suggesting, by implication at least, the dangers of theological controversy and conflict. Such people immediately don their asbestos suits of theological orthodoxy, determining that they will judiciously avoid the flames of fanaticism and the sparks of sensationalism.

Others, eager for new and novel spiritual experiences, grasp at these words as a drowning man grasps at a straw. In their extremity, they use these words as a label to describe unorthodox interpretations of Scripture and questionable expeditions into the realm of the mystical and emotional. In their zeal they proceed to offer "false fire" on the altar of their hearts, identifying the vagaries of their abnormal experiences as valid New Testament Christianity. This, however, is the "wild fire" of fanaticism, that allures its followers like a will-o'-the-wisp onto the marsh land of subjective emotions and feelings.

To others again, dissatisfied with the "no fire" of formalism and leery of the "wild fire" of fanaticism, these words suggest an intervention of God in the affairs and activities of men, such as brings profound conviction of sin and permanent conversion to righteousness. The phrase, indeed, has become a synonym for revival, and many believers today are crying in their hearts for a fresh manifestation of the "true fire" of the Lord. Such a manifestation, they are convinced, is an absolute necessity if the church is to make an impact on a secular and sinful society.

But if we are to derive maximum benefits from our study of the power of revival, it is necessary that we consider the words *the fire of the Lord* both with regard to their original context and to their precise meaning.

Undoubtedly, they are right who see in the reference to the fire of the Lord the focal point of the dramatic account of 1 Kings 18. In these words we come clearly to the climax of the contest between Elijah and the prophets of Baal. Most certainly it was the advent and activity of the fire of the Lord that settled for the people the question as to the identity of the true and living God. By the coming of the fire, in answer to Elijah's plea, Jehovah was seen to be "the God that answereth by fire," the true and living God (18:24).

It is this distinguishing capacity of fire that gives us a key to its symbolism. The fire falling from above bore testimony to the veracity and validity of the prophet's claims. It became the symbol of reality in relation to spiritual matters. It marked out that which was true from that which was false and specious.

Search the Scriptures, and you will find this explanation of the meaning of the heavenly fire substantiated in many places. In the tabernacle and the temple, the fire was the token of God's presence in the midst of Israel. In the case of David, after his repentance over his sin in numbering the people, the Lord "answered him from heaven by fire upon the altar of burnt offering" (1 Ch 21:26). And on the day of Pentecost, the descending Spirit was symbolized by tongues like as of fire (Ac 2:3).

With this key in our hand, let us proceed to open the chapter from which our text is taken. The church as a whole needs to be brought to a Mount Carmel crisis. There needs to be a spiritual and moral showdown. Voices are being raised, demanding demonstration of the reality of our claims that the gospel is the answer to man's problems and that God is alive, not dead.

Our text reads, "Then the fire of the LORD fell." When was "then"? What preceded the advent of the fire from heaven? What made it possible for God to send the fire? Or, dropping the striking symbolism for a moment lest the point be missed, when can we today expect the presence of God in power to be manifested in our churches and in our lives? Are there any conditions to be met?

Let us look at the teaching of 1 Kings 18.

ISSUE CLARIFIED

The fire of the Lord fell when the issue, basic to the entire situation facing Israel, was clarified. For this aspect, let us pick up the story in 1 Kings 18:17. Ahab, king of Israel, had just met Elijah, God's prophet, who, three years before, had announced a devastating drought to come upon the land. Ahab had in no way been softened through the divine judgment; rather, he was belligerent and caustic. His first words to Elijah, were, "Art thou he that troubleth Israel?"

Ahab attributed the cause of the drought to Elijah. If you had asked the king what was the real issue, he would have responded that it was the meddling of the prophet in the affairs of the nation.

But Elijah was ready with his answer. "I have not troubled Israel," was his reply, "but thou, and thy father's house, in that ye have forsaken the commandments of the Lord, and thou hast followed Baalim."

Ask Elijah the nature of the real issue, and he would answer, "The backsliding of the leaders of the nation. The leaders have fallen into a ditch, and the people have tumbled in after them. The real problem is the rebellion and apostasy of the leaders."

Elijah did not seek to curry favor with the king; he boldly confronted Ahab with the real issue, sharply rebuking the king for his disloyalty to Jehovah.

We may affirm it as a basic principle of revival that the fire of the Lord is preceded by a time when men and women honestly face the real issues. There needs to be a prophetic word spoken to us—probing, piercing, and pressing us to our knees.

Many are the proposals being made concerning the cause of the church's barrenness, many of them missing the mark entirely. We are told that the church's message is no longer relevant; that the church's ministry ought to include social work; that old truths must be presented by new techniques. The proposals are legion, but are they really speaking to the issue?

To Elijah the issue was but single and simple: Ahab had backslid. The drought was not due to a temporary cessation of the moisture in the atmosphere over the land of Palestine. (That's how the experts would have defined it!) Jehovah had locked up the heavens because Ahab had sinned!

In our hearts, too, we know the real cause of our barrenness and weakness. We need to be confronted by a prophet-like man of God who will put his finger directly and definitely on the source of our problems. When he comes, there will be no escaping him.

INDECISION CHALLENGED

As we have seen, the fire of the Lord fell when the issue had been clarified, but note that it was also when *the* indecision of the people had been challenged. Elijah commanded (right—commanded!) Ahab to gather all the people of Israel for a confrontation with the prophet on the slopes of Mount Carmel. Elijah asked also for the presence of the four hundred and fifty prophets of Baal and the four hundred prophets of the groves, whom Ahab's wife Jezebel personally supported.

There on Mount Carmel, Elijah challenged the indecision of the people. Here are his words: "How long halt ye between two opinions? If the LORD be God, follow Him: but if Baal, then follow him." Elijah described the people of Israel as standing at the crossroads, unable—or unwilling—to make a final decision. First, they went down one road; then they went back up and tried the other. They shilly-shallied between serving Jehovah and the Baals.

Elijah's trenchant challenge, then, was aimed at bringing to an end the indecision of the people. They could not serve two masters. They must decide between Jehovah and the Baals.

Is it not substantially true to say that Elijah's graphic description of a people at the crossroads, hesitating and holding back from a total commitment to either way, is an accurate portrayal of many "Christians" today? Someone has remarked that there are Christians who know enough of the joys of the Christian life to make the pleasures of this world empty, but they do not know enough of the joys of the Christian life to be done with the pleasures of this world once and for all.

Consider the following aspects of the crime of Israel's indecision:

They were undecided when an ungodly king was bent on leading them into idolatry.

They were undecided even though they were experiencing a divine judgment upon their land on account of their sins.

They were undecided when the true prophets of the Lord were being massacred and martyred.

They were undecided when the truth of God's law was being opposed and denied.

And is our indecision any less serious? Has not God spoken once, yea, twice, to our generation? But we have chosen to disregard His warnings and to ignore the danger signals.

IDOLATRY EXPOSED

The fire of the Lord fell when the issue had been clarified and when the indecision of the people had been challenged. But we learn from the account in 1 Kings 18 that it also fell when the idolatry of the priests of Baal had been exposed for what it really was—empty, hollow deception.

The prophets of Baal and the prophets of the grove had apparently gained great prominence in the religious life of Israel. With their pomp and their pageantry, they had established a name for themselves. Now Elijah is concerned with exposing the folly of idolatry before the people.

To the people, therefore, Elijah proposed a simple contest. Let the four-hundred-fifty prophets of Baal—vastly superior in number to Jehovah's lone prophet—prepare a bullock for sacrifice but light no fire under the animal once it was laid upon the altar. Elijah would do likewise. Then, declared Elijah, let the prophets of Baal call on their gods and he would call on the name of Jehovah, "And the God that answereth by fire, let him be God" (18:24).

102

As we have mentioned already, it was the fire that was to demonstrate whose God was really alive and able to intervene. The fire would be the seal and the sign of reality.

To this proposal, the people gave agreement, and the ceremonies began. In 1 Kings 18:25-29, we are given a step-by-step description of the activities of the prophets of Baal. They dressed their bullock, they called on Baal, they danced frantically around their altar, but it was all to no avail. From morning until midafternoon, they continued their feverish activities, but there was no answer. No fire appeared to consume the sacrifice. Baal had been exposed as being a figment of their imagination and the product of their own desires and designs.

We do not wish at this point to institute an illegitimate comparison between the priests of Baal and those in religious work today, but there are some applications of this scene in 1 Kings 18 that may be made.

The priests of Baal were guilty of worshiping a false god. The first application, therefore, is whom are you serving? Is it the God of revelation, the God and Father of our Lord Jesus Christ, or is it a god of your own fashioning and fabrication? Many, including ministers within the organized church, are guilty of worshiping false gods—the gods of popularity, of success, or of acceptance.

Second, the priests of Baal were guilty of misdirected effort. They sacrificed, they prayed, they danced, they cut themselves, but nothing happened. Here is zeal aplenty, but no results. That, we believe, is a picture of many a person engaged in so-called Christian work. There is sacrifice, there is praying, there is the expending of one's energy, there is zeal, but so often there is no result.

Third, the priests of Baal were guilty of an empty professionalism. They wore the garments, they chanted the songs, they knew the ritual, but their whole ministry was characterized by professionalism, void of reality and of results.

103

Let me emphasize the point again: the fire of the Lord fell when the idolatry of the professionals was exposed. And surely we need something like this in the church today. There are too many who profess to serve the true God who, in reality, are serving false gods. The fire of the Lord will fall when there has been a drastic exposure of such hirelings.

INSTRUCTION CONVEYED

As we have noticed, the fire of the Lord fell after the issue had been clarified, after the indecision of the people had been challenged, after the idolatry of the priests had been exposed. Now let us look at the fact that the fire of the Lord fell when the instruction of the prophet had been conveyed to the people.

Let us picture the scene. The prophets of Baal are standing beside their altar, exhausted, sullen, and frustrated. Now Elijah bids the people to gather around him. He builds the altar of the Lord, which for years has been in a state of disrepair. He purposely builds the altar out of twelve large stones, one for each of the twelve tribes of Israel. He then digs a deep trench around the altar. He next prepares the bullock for the sacrifice and lays it on the altar.

Then, to the amazement of the people, he gives commands for four barrels to be filled with water and for the water to be poured on the sacrifice. Three times he gives instructions for this to be done, until the trench is filled to the brim.

Now, it is important to grasp that Elijah was using this entire procedure as a visual aid to instruct the people. He soaked the sacrifice with water in order to show that it would be impossible for him to light the sacrifice himself. If the sacrifice were to be consumed, it would have to be consumed now by a miracle of God. The fire that could dramatically burn the sacrifice could be only from the Lord.

In so doing, of course, Elijah was stepping out in faith. He wanted to make it crystal clear that he was totally dependent upon Jehovah for an answer. He had no gadgets or gimmicks up his sleeve to fall back on if God failed him. He had no alternative numbers on his program if no fire fell. It was the fire of Jehovah or nothing. And thereby he teaches us that God's eternal decree is that no flesh should glory in His presence.

When the fire of the Lord did fall from heaven, the people did not chant Elijah's praises; rather, "They fell on their faces, and they said, The LORD, he is the God; the LORD, he is the God" (1 Ki 18:39).

We draw attention to the fact that Elijah was not passive; he made due preparations. He was active up to a point. But there came a moment when he wanted it to be recognized by his audience that he was no expert in pyrotechnics, able at will to kindle a miraculous fire. He wanted them to know that he was not, like the priests of Baal, a charlatan, seeking to dupe and delude them.

What a message is here for modern evangelism! How would some of our professional evangelists have handled the situation that Elijah faced? Elijah had no advertising agents out announcing, "Come and see the greatest fire-maker of all time—never seen in public before!" He was no showman, attempting to turn the contest into a circus.

Perhaps the greatest barrier to revival on a large scale is the fact that we are too interested in a great display. We want an exhibition; God is looking for a man who will throw himself entirely on God.

Whenever self-effort, self-glory, self-seeking, or self-promotion enters into the work of revival, then God leaves us to ourselves. The scene on Mount Carmel teaches us that ultimately, revival is not originated by man, but by God. It is the fire of the Lord and not of man that consumes the sacrifice.

Are we in the place where, having done our part, we are seeking that demonstration of God's power in our midst that

105

will confirm the reality of our claims that God is alive and concerned about men and women?

Our final observation is to the effect that "the fire of the Lord" fell when intercession had been made.

Let's quote the Scripture at this point. "And it came to pass at the time of the offering of the evening sacrifice, that Elijah the prophet came near, and said, LORD God of Abraham, Isaac, and of Israel, let it be known this day that thou art God in Israel, and that I am thy servant, and that I have done all these things at thy word. Hear me, O LORD, hear me, that this people may know that thou art the LORD God, and that thou hast turned their heart back again" (18:36-37).

Here is prayer that was the heart cry of a man righteous before God (Ja 5:17-18).

Here is prayer that was the prayer of a man of faith.

Here is prayer that was the desire of a man who was concerned about the glory of God alone.

Here is prayer that was expectant and that anticipated God's answer.

Here is prayer that was definite and to the point.

This prayer deserves fuller study than we have space for here, but we would call attention to the very next statement in the account. Prayer was offered, and, "Then the fire of the LORD fell and consumed the burnt-sacrifice, and the wood, and the stones, and the dust, and licked up the water that was in the trench" (18:38).

What a display! What a demonstration! God intervened, and that fire proved to all the waiting people that Jehovah was the true God.

How shall we convince men and women of the reality of God in our lives? Get on fire! Prayed George Whitefield, "May Jesus make me and all His ministers a flaming fire."

TRUE AND FALSE ZEAL

Zeal is that pure and heavenly flame
    The fire of love supplies;
While that which often bears the name
    Is self in a disguise.

True zeal is merciful and mild,
    Can pity and forbear;
The false is headstrong, fierce, and wild,
    And breathes revenge and war.

While zeal for truth the Christian warms,
    He knows the worth of peace;
But self contends for names and forms,
    Its party to increase.

Zeal has attain'd its highest aim,
    Its end is satisfied,
If sinners love the Saviour's name;
    Nor seeks it aught beside.

But self, however well employ'd,
    Has its own ends in view;
And says, as boasting Jehu cried,
    'Come, see what I can do!'

Dear Lord, the idol self dethrone,
    And from our hearts remove;
And let no zeal by us be shown
    But that which springs from love.

JOHN NEWTON

THE PERIL OF REVIVAL

*And Nadab and Abihu, the sons of Aaron, took
either of them his censer, and put fire therein, and
put incense thereon, and offered strange fire before
the Lord, which he commanded them not.*

*And there went out fire from the Lord, and
devoured them, and they died before the Lord.*
LEVITICUS 10:1-2

IN TIMES OF REVIVAL, God's people, especially their leaders,
must be on guard lest there be introduced into their spiritual
exercises an element of "false fire," either in the form of
carnal zeal or fleshly methods.

This is the paramount peril of revival.

In the book of Leviticus there is recorded for us an incident containing much in the way of warning and direction
as we seek for definite manifestations of God's presence in
our midst. It is the incident involving Nadab and Abihu,
sons of Aaron, the Israelite high priest.

Before we turn to examine the account, there are two
points that should be constantly kept in mind as we seek the
explanation of the happenings recorded for us there.

First, when we are studying the tabernacle system or any
part of it—the building itself, the priesthood, the sacrifices,
or the feasts—then we must keep in mind that all the forms
and features of the system were divinely revealed. It was
Jehovah Himself who dictated and determined the method
whereby His people could approach Him. Every detail of the

system was revealed and regulated by the Lord—the laver, burnt offering, the offering of incense, the altar of shewbread, the lampstand, the ark, and the mercy seat. Nothing was left to the imagination or initiative of Moses or Aaron. There were rules for the transportation of the tabernacle and its furniture. In fact, there were rules for the priests to observe with regard to every aspect of the tabernacle system.

Second, we must recognize that for anyone to disregard the arrangements and requirements set forth by the Lord constituted an act of presumption against the authority of their divine King. For a priest to arbitrarily change or arrogantly modify any of the divine specifications was to commit willful sin against God. Jehovah not only revealed the way of approach to His throne, He also jealously regulated that way, in order that He might be held in honor and holiness before His people.

We turn now to study the account of Nadab and Abihu in order that its lessons and warnings might ever be kept in mind as we seek for the glory of the Lord to be manifested in our midst. The account is found in Leviticus 10:1-7.

THE INCIDENT

Let us begin by seeking to grasp the salient features of the incident itself. It is important that we read and understand the account as given to us in the Scriptures.

The story really begins in Leviticus 8. There we read that the Lord said to Moses, "Take Aaron and his sons with him, and the garments, and the anointing oil, and a bullock for the sin offering, and two rams, and a basket of unleavened bread; and gather thou all the congregation together unto the door of the tabernacle of the congregation" (8:2-3).

These verses remind us that the context of the story concerning Nadab and Abihu is that of the consecration and commissioning of the Aaronic priesthood, a very solemn and sacred event in the history of Israel.

The remaining part of Leviticus 8 records how Moses did as the Lord commanded (Indeed, this is the keynote of both chaps. 8 and 9; see, e.g., 8:4-5, 9, 13, 17, 21, 29, 34, 35-36; 9:6-7, 21).

After the initial rites had been performed by Moses upon Aaron and his sons, those newly consecrated to the Lord's service and glory were commanded to stay inside the tabernacle area for seven days (8:31-36).

On the eighth day—the day which in Old Testament typology prefigured the day of Christ's resurrection and the commencement of a new era—special ceremonies were to be undertaken with reference to Aaron (Lev 9:2) and the people (9:3-4). It was after these ceremonies, involving the sin, burnt, meal, and peace offerings that we read, "Aaron lifted up his hand toward the people, and blessed them, and came down from offering of the sin offering, and the burnt offering, and peace offerings. And Moses and Aaron went into the tabernacle of the congregation, and came out, and blessed the people: and the glory of the LORD appeared unto all the people. And there came a fire out from before the LORD, and consumed upon the altar the burnt offering and the fat: which when all the people saw, they shouted, and fell on their faces" (9:22-24).

This was the climax and culmination of the entire eight days of ceremony. God's people saw both "the glory of the LORD" and "the fire of the LORD" and were awed in the Lord's presence.

With this as a general background, we are ready now to investigate the account of Nadab and Abihu and their sin of willful presumption in their relationship to God.

First, consider the inauguration they beheld. Chapter 10 follows chapter 9 immediately in the sequence of time, so that we must keep in mind the entire proceedings of chapter 9 as we study chapter 10. In chapter 9, the focus is upon the work and ministry of Aaron the high priest, as typical of

111

Christ the great High Priest. It is his day, and it was God's will that he should be preeminent in it. The spotlight was not shared by his sons. They appeared entirely in a secondary capacity.

But note, second, the initiative they took. In Leviticus 10:1 we read, "Nadab and Abihu, the sons of Aaron, took either of them his censer, and put fire therein, and put incense thereon." For some reason, acting as a team, these two sons of Aaron decided to have a part in the ceremonies of that day and so prepared their incense censers to offer the fragrant incense before the Lord.

Third, we note the incense they offered. "Nadab and Abihu . . . offered strange fire before the Lord, which he commanded them not." It would seem that this offering of incense was made outside the sanctuary itself, probably in the courtyard in front of the main gate into the tabernacle area. Thus it would have been in the sight of all the people.

Fourth, we note the impiety they manifested. On the basis of 10:3, we may say that Nadab and Abihu in their conduct did not sanctify the Lord and did not glorify Him before all the people. Their actions and attitudes were grossly impious and irreverent. As one writer commented,

> As they perished not within the Tabernacle, but in front of it, it seems likely that they may have been making an ostentatious and irreverent display of their ministration to accompany the shouts of the people. . . . The offence for which they were immediately visited with outward punishment was thus a flagrant outrage on the solemn order of the divine service, while the cause of their offence may have been their guilty excess.[1]

Finally, we note the indignation they aroused. "There went out fire from the Lord, and devoured them, and they died before the Lord. Then Moses said unto Aaron, This is it that the Lord spake, saying, I will be sanctified in them that come nigh me, and before all the people I will be glori-

fied. And Aaron held his peace" (10:2-3). There, then, is
the account of the incident.

THE INTERPRETATION

We are concerned now to seek the interpretation of this
event, which climaxed, as we have seen, in severe judgment.
While commentators are by no means agreed with regard to
the details of the story, let us try to understand the event
from the standpoint first of the motive of Nadab and Abihu
and then with regard to the method employed by these two
sons of Aaron.

First, then, consider the motive of these two men. What
prompted Nadab and Abihu in their willful act of presumption? Here we can but suggest reasons.

Were Nadab and Abihu motivated by a desire to share the
limelight with Aaron and Moses? Were they peeved that they
had no major part in the wonderful events of that day? Were
they determined to play a leading role, even though it be
anticlimactic to the appearance of the glory and the fire of
the Lord? Did they want to put on a display before the people so that they, too, would be held in high honor?

Or were they drunk? Strange suggestion, you say? But read
the very next section in Leviticus 10. With what does it deal?
The total abstinence of the priests! We read, "The LORD
spake unto Aaron [note that unusual statement; the Lord
generally gave instructions to Moses] saying, Do not drink
wine nor strong drink, thou, nor thy sons with thee, when
ye go into the tabernacle of the congregation, lest ye die: it
shall be a statute forever throughout your generations: and
that ye may put difference between holy and unholy, and between unclean and clean" (10:8-10).

It is highly significant that these instructions appear at this
juncture of the story. We are forced to relate the commands
concerning abstinence to the event of 10:1-7. For seven days,
the priests would have had no opportunity to drink either

113

wine or strong drink. Had Nadab and Abihu been drinking on the eighth day just prior to their act of impiety? The evidence seems to point to that conclusion.

The picture, then, that emerges is this: at a moment of great excitement, when God's people were awed by the manifestation of God's glory and fire, two priests, consecrated representatives of the people, yet drunk with wine, proceeded to act in a way that brought dishonor to God.

But what now of their method? The following suggestions may help to pinpoint the seriousness of their sin in God's sight.

First, the occasion did not require the offering of incense. God's glory, the symbol of His presence, and God's fire, the symbol of His pleasure, had just appeared to the people. There was no need at that moment for man to intervene and offer incense.

Again, the focus was upon Aaron. God had given him the priority on that day. His sons should have been content to play a secondary role.

There is no evidence from Scripture that incense was to be offered by two priests. Because of the symbolical and typical character of the priest as he offered incense, the ministry was undertaken by one individual (e.g., Lk 1:8-10).

Because of the reference to "strange fire," it would seem that the incense was lit not by fire from the altar of burnt offering (as was required on special occasions, perhaps even every day). Indeed, it would seem from Leviticus 16:1-2 that the death of Nadab and Abihu was made the occasion for further instruction to Aaron by the Lord with regard to the way of approach. In that chapter we read, "He [Aaron] shall take a censer full of burning coals of fire from off the altar before the Lord" for the ceremonies on the day of atonement (16:12).

Although it is true that the incense offered to the Lord was to be made according to a divine prescription (Ex 30:34-38), we are on more debatable ground if we maintain that the incense offered by Nadab and Abihu itself was illegal. This does not seem to be the emphasis of Leviticus 10.

THE INSTRUCTION

We have studied the incident involving the offering of strange fire by Nadab and Abihu; we have sought to find an interpretation for it both in the area of their motive and their method; now let us seek to apply this entire incident to ourselves today.

As a background for our application, let us bear in mind the occasion of the sin of Nadab and Abihu. It was when God was manifesting Himself to His people as the true God and as their triumphant King. Always at such times there is danger that some among His people, leaders in particular, will offer strange fire to the Lord.

But, you may ask, *specifically* how may we offer strange fire?

Here are four ways.

We offer strange fire to the Lord when we promote some scheme or idea of our own in total disregard and defiance of the Word of God. The evidence, as we have seen, points to the fact that Nadab and Abihu were not ruled by the divine Word. There were clear regulations prohibiting what they did.

The lesson here for us is that we must be constantly in subjection to the Word of God in all our worship, service, and work. While it is true that we do not have a manual of rules and regulations similar to the Levitical system, there are principles and procedures given in God's Word to regulate us in all our activities.

Second, we offer strange fire to the Lord when we serve with an exaggerated sense of our own authority. As Dr. Oswald Allis stated, "The incident is a solemn warning against every sin of presumption, self-assertion, and levity."[2]

115

Nadab and Abihu were disgruntled that they had been ignored in the day's proceedings. They determined to get into the act and did it by intruding into the sacred ritual.

We say it with sadness—and yet it must be said—there are those in Christian work who are puffed up by pride and who strut about seeking the praise of men, not the praise of God. They undertake various projects, not because they feel it is the will of God, but rather because they will receive the applause and acclamation of men.

Third, we offer strange fire to the Lord when we serve in the energy of the flesh rather than in the energy of the Spirit. As mentioned earlier, Nadab and Abihu were probably drunk when they acted impiously. Right to the point, therefore, is the apostolic admonition, "Be not drunk with wine, wherein is excess; but be filled with the Spirit" (Eph 5:18). While wine in this reference does refer to the literal intoxicant, it may also be the symbol of all that adversely controls men in their carnal ambitions.

There is the wine of intellectual achievement. That is a wine which spurs men on to win their case and to glory in their mental dexterity and ability. F. W. Farrar wrote concerning "the unhallowed fire of false argument on the sacred altar of truth."

There is the wine of emotional response. How many get drunk at this point! Indeed, some have come to equate genuine Christianity with something which they describe as "liquid fire running up and down the spine." That, we believe, is perilously close to offering strange fire. We need to hear Paul saying firmly and finally, "We are the circumcision, which worship God in the spirit, and rejoice in Christ Jesus, and have no confidence in the flesh" (Phil 3:3).

Finally, we believe that it is possible to offer strange fire when we substitute the fire of our own igniting for the fire of the Lord. This, in essence, is what Nadab and Abihu did.

They disregarded the fire of the Lord burning on the altar of sacrifice and kindled their own fire in order to burn incense.

George Williams explained the significance of this: "Their fire had therefore no connection with the atonement . . . Acceptable worship can only be in the energy of the Spirit, in the truth of the shed Blood, and in obedience to the inspired Word. The fire of the Holy Spirit associated itself alone with the Blood of the crucified Saviour; all other fire is 'strange fire.' "[3]

The Salvation Army has as its motto "Blood and Fire." In these days of confusion, we must make sure that our worship and service are based both on the blood of Christ and on the fire of the Holy Spirit.

At the extreme southwestern tip of Italy there is a twofold danger for seamen. On the one hand, there is a dangerous rock known as Scylla; on the other, opposite the rock, is a whirlpool known as Charybdis. The mariner faces twin dangers as he seeks to steer his boat in that region.

So it is in things spiritual. There is the dangerous rock known as "No Fire." There is the dangerous whirlpool known as "False Fire." We believe that it is possible for the believer to chart a course between these two dangers that will bring him to his desired haven without wreck or ruin. It is a way that is true to the Scriptures and that results in the greater glory of God.

117

HEAR US, O SAVIOUR!

Hear us, O Saviour, while we pray,
    Humbly our need confessing;
Grant us the promis'd show'rs today—
    Send them upon us, O Lord!

Knowing Thy love, on Thee we call,
    Boldly Thy throne addressing;
Pleading that show'rs of grace may fall—
    Send them upon us, O Lord!

Trusting Thy word that cannot fail,
    Master, we claim Thy promise,
Oh that our faith may now prevail—
    Send us the showers, O Lord!

    Send show'rs of blessing;
    Send show'rs refreshing;
    Send us show'rs of blessing;
    Send them, Lord, we pray!

FANNY J. CROSBY

11

THE PRINCIPLE OF REVIVAL

I will cause the shower to come down in his season; there shall be showers of blessing. EZEKIEL 34:26

"WE MUST HAVE REVIVAL. It must rain faster, or we perish with drought!" So claimed Dr. Lyman Beecher during the last century. What exactly did he mean? How do we explain his reference to rain?

For an explanation we must turn to the Old Testament. In relationship to the land of Palestine, the withholding of rain was a sign and seal of God's judgment upon Israel. Before their entrance into the promised land, a land which drank "water of the rain of heaven" (Deu 11:11), Moses warned the people that if they sinned against the Lord, the Lord would make the rain of their land to be powder and dust (Deu 28:24).

That form of judgment was carried out repeatedly in Israel's history. Elijah, for example, as the prophet of the Lord, announced, "As the LORD God of Israel liveth, before whom I stand, there shall not be dew nor rain these years, but according to my word" (1 Ki 17:1).

On the other hand, whenever God's people repented and returned to Jehovah, then there was abundant rain upon the land. After the dramatic showdown on Mount Carmel, when the people of Israel acknowledged that Jehovah is God, "The heaven was black with clouds and wind, and there was a great rain" (1 Ki 18:45).

119

With this historical and geographical background, we are able to see that by analogy, the ministry of the Holy Spirit is compared to rain from heaven. When the believer is obedient to God's Word, the Holy Spirit works graciously and effectively in his heart; when he is disobedient, the Holy Spirit's blessing is withheld. While, therefore, we recognize that in many of the passages we refer to, literal rain is meant, we feel that we in no way violate the general teaching of Scripture by applying these references to spiritual blessing.

Our whole subject is summed up beautifully in Ezekiel 34:20-31. It is in this portion that we find the well-known phrase, "showers of blessing." We quote from verse 26: "I will cause the shower to come down in his season; there shall be showers of blessing."

"Showers of blessing"—what a wonderful promise! Let us relate it to the ministry of the Holy Spirit in our hearts. We can best clarify and classify our thoughts by considering first, the need for such showers of blessing; second, the promise of such showers; and, third, the results of such showers.

THE NEED

Consider the need for such showers of blessing as intimated in our text. As we study the general biblical context of this wonderful promise, we discover that various aspects of the need are emphasized.

First, it is only through such showers that we can present God's ideal for His people in the world. God's ideal for His people is clearly stated in the passage, "I will make them and the places round about my hill a blessing" (34:26). God's ideal for His people, simply stated, is that they may be a channel of blessing to others.

This is implicit in the promise given to Abraham: "I will bless thee, . . . and thou shalt be a blessing" (Gen 12:2). Far too often, we pray to be blessed by God, but we never relate that blessing to others. But according to God's Word, we are to be blessed in order that we may bless others. We are both to receive and to relay God's blessing. We are not called to be containers but conveyors of spiritual refreshment.

Second, it is only through such showers of blessing, symbolic of the Spirit's ministry, that we can prevent a total drought and stop the church in the twentieth century from becoming a dust bowl.

On one occasion, Ezekiel the prophet had to state emphatically concerning the land of Palestine, "Thou art the land that is not . . . rained upon in the day of indignation" (Eze 22:24). And what of the church today? Are we not suffering from a drought that threatens to turn the church into a dust bowl—a dry, barren wilderness? Oh, how we need showers of blessing to prevent such a tragedy continuing!

Third, it is only when the church receives showers of blessing that we can produce a harvest. God's Word exhorts us, "Sow to yourselves in righteousness, reap in mercy" (Ho 10:12); but how shall we reap without previous showers of blessing? If the desert of our world is to blossom as the rose, then it is upon God's people that the refreshing, reviving showers must first fall.

In Joel's day, there was a massive drought that paralyzed the entire agricultural activity of the nation. At that time, Joel was sent with a message of repentance, and when God's people heeded the warning, Joel was able to say, "Be glad then, ye children of Zion, and rejoice in the Lord your God: for he hath given you the former rain moderately, and he will cause to come down for you the rain, the former rain, and the latter rain in the first month" (Joel 2:23).

If we are dry and barren in our hearts, it is only as we repent that we can receive the fructifying showers of blessing that will in turn guarantee a harvest of spiritual fruit.

Our local churches need the showers of blessing. Pastors, evangelists, and missionaries need showers of blessing. Sun-

121

day school teachers and youth workers need showers of blessing. Christian parents and Christians of all ages need showers
of blessing. Indeed, as we contemplate the desperate need for
these divinely promised showers of blessing, we are constrain-
ed to cry out,

> Breathe, O mighty Breath from Heaven,
> On earth's dry and parched plains;
> Send the wind-swept clouds before us,
> Deluging the earth with rains.

HERBERT TOVY
Used by permission of
Eva M. Tovy

THE PROMISE

Shall we stress the need any further? Are we not convinced in our hearts that we need showers of blessing? Consider, then, the promise of showers of blessing. God announced to His people, "I will cause the showers to come
down in his season; there shall be showers of blessing."

This promise reminds us that there are divine resources
available to meet divine requirements. Hosea the prophet,
whom we have just quoted, goes on in his stirring challenge
to say, "Sow to yourselves in righteousness, reap in mercy;
break up your fallow ground: for it is time to seek the LORD,
till He come and rain righteousness upon you" (10:12).
There is our hope: the intervention of the Lord Himself in
sending rain upon us. "Drop down, ye heavens, from above,
and let the skies pour down righteousness" (Is 45:8).

This divine promise, "There shall be showers of blessing,"
must be seen as one of a series of promises given to God's
people. Initially, the promise was given to Israel and will be
fulfilled, we believe, in a literal fashion when Israel is restored to the land. Then the land of Palestine will again become the garden land of the whole earth.

There is a principle embodied in the promise of showers of blessing that we may apply to God's people today. Taken in this way, Ezekiel's phrase, indeed, may be looked upon as equivalent to Peter's phrase in Acts 3:19, "Times of refreshing . . . from the presence of the Lord."

It will be profitable for us to look briefly at the series of promises given to Israel in Ezekiel 34, of which the promise of showers of blessing is one.

First, there is the promise of judgment upon false leaders of Israel (Eze 34:20-22). What a solemn word is this to all who profess to be shepherds of God's flock (cf. 1 Pe 5:1-4)! God has a controversy with those who have mismanaged and mistreated His sheep. (See Ez 34:1-9 for a catalog of their crimes.) Before there can be blessing, there must be judgment upon those who have misled God's sheep.

Second, there is the promise of government for God's people. "I will set up one shepherd over them, and he shall feed them" (34:23). Surely God has appointed the Lord Jesus Christ, David's greater Son, to be the head over all things to the church (34:24). "He shall be their shepherd," is the divine word. God not only removes false shepherds; He appoints a true Shepherd over His flock.

Third, there is the promise of enjoyment of God's covenant. "I will make with them a covenant of peace, and will cause the evil beasts to cease out of the land: and they shall dwell safely in the wilderness, and sleep in the woods" (34:25). Here is pictured a people whose trust is completely in God. As the Shepherd of the sheep, He protects His own from wild beasts so that they may sleep without fear in the wilderness or the woods, that is, anywhere they may find themselves.

It is after these promises—judgment, government, and enjoyment—have been introduced that the promise is given concerning refreshment: "I will cause the showers to come down in his season; there shall be showers of blessing."

It is very rare in Scripture that a promise of blessing appears without context or condition. One problem inherent in promise box method of selecting a verse for the day is that in most cases, the context and the conditions of the promise are ignored. We have taken time in this study to review the setting of the promise of showers of blessing in order that we might see how it fits into God's plan. It is where there is judgment of that which is wrong and the recognition of Christ's government in the church that God can send showers of blessing upon His people.

This promise, therefore, must be seen as one in a series of divine promises. But it must also be supported by other promises of a similar nature found in other passages.

Such showers of blessing are assured by the Lord: "Prove me now herewith, saith the LORD of hosts, if I will not open you the windows of heaven, and pour you out a blessing" (Mal 3:10).

Such showers of blessing are abundant: "I will pour water upon him that is thirsty, and floods upon the dry ground" (Is 44:3).

Such showers of blessing are adequate to meet our need: "Thou, O God, didst send a plentiful rain, whereby thou didst confirm thine inheritance, when it was weary" (Ps 68:9).

Finally, we note that this promise of showers of blessing must be sought in faith.

There is here an important principle. In Ezekiel 36, after disclosing His program for Israel, the Lord asserted, "I will yet for this be enquired of by the house of Israel, to do it for them" (36:37). This verse teaches us that there is nothing mechanical or magical about the fulfillment of God's promises. They are brought to pass through the prayers of His people.

In the light of this principle, we would affirm that the "showers of blessing" do not come to us routinely, but in answer to very definite praying on the part of the church.

In one of his books, Dr. A. B. Simpson tells us of a child who was asked what appropriating faith is and who gave this answer, "It is taking a pencil and underscoring the *me*s and *mine*s and *my*s in the Bible."[1] While the child may not be hermeneutically correct, his answer points to the fact that we must appropriate what God has given. One poet put the truth this way:

> There shall be showers of blessing;
> Send them upon us, O Lord;
> Grant to us now a refreshing,
> Come and now honour Thy Word.
>
> DANIEL W. WHITTLE

The principle of asking and appropriating, then, must be followed. Does God promise "showers of blessing?" Then I must fervently, frequently, and faithfully seek His face for the bestowment of His blessing. I too must pray,

> Lord, I hear of showers of blessings
> Thou art scattering full and free;
> Showers the thirsty land refreshing;
> Let some drops now fall on me.
>
> ELIZABETH A. CODNER

THE RESULTS

We have examined the need for such showers of blessing as promised by the Lord, and how real that need is. We have studied the divine promise of showers of blessing and how it fills our hearts with hope. We must now give careful attention to the results of these showers of blessing.

When we experience "showers of blessing," there is reviving, growth, and fruitfulness.

First, when the showers of blessing fall, there is reviving:

125

There shall be showers of blessing:
Precious reviving again;
Over the hills and the valleys,
Sound of abundance of rain.

DANIEL W. WHITTLE

People who live on the prairies have often seen the fields around them begin to wither and dry up from lack of rain. Days filled with concern for the farmers have come and gone, and then at last the rains have come. What a reviving there is when the showers have fallen! Fields begin to grow green again, and there is the promise of harvest.

How tragic that Christians should be content with their dry and dusty spiritual condition! How pitiful are those who never give a glance to the horizon to see if there is a cloud even the size of a man's hand! Our only hope of reviving is the showers of blessing promised by God.

Showers promote growth. Where plants have been stunted through the lack of moisture, the rains accelerate growth. There is a wonderful word picture of growth given in Hosea 14:5-7. Concerning Israel, it is written, "He shall grow as the lily, and cast forth his roots as Lebanon. His branches shall spread, and his beauty shall be as the olive tree, and his smell as Lebanon. They that dwell under His shadow shall return; they shall revive as the corn, and grow as the vine: the scent thereof shall be as the wine of Lebanon."

Here reviving and growth are joined together. Get revived, and you grow as a Christian.

Along with reviving and growth, showers produce a harvest. We have quoted from Malachi 3:10 already. God promises to open the windows of heaven to faith, then He states: "I will . . . pour you out a blessing, that there shall not be room enough to receive it." That means there will be such an abundant harvest that the barns will not be big enough to hold the produce.

126

Does someone say, "But the days of revival are over?" Rather, should we not say, "The days of men and women crying out for revival are over"? Let us read again the account of Elijah on Mount Carmel. Although there was not a cloud in the azure sky, the prophet could say in faith, "There is a sound of abundance of rain" (1 Ki 18:41). And although his servant reported six times that he could see nothing on the horizon, Elijah believed that God's faithfulness was such that showers would inevitably come inasmuch as Israel had turned nationally to Jehovah in repentance. Finally, there came out of the sea a little cloud, like a man's hand. Soon the heaven was black with clouds and wind, and there was a great rain.

We may be dry. We may not see much in the way of showers of blessing. But if our hearts are seeking God's face, if we are laying hold of His promise, and if we believe that the God of Elijah is still alive today, then there will yet be a deluge of blessing upon the church of Christ.

> God is here, and that to bless us
> With the Spirit's quickening power;
> See, the cloud, already bending,
> Waits to drop the grateful shower.

JAMES L. BLACK

"Then shall we know, if we follow on to know the Lord: his going forth is prepared as the morning; and he shall come unto us as the rain, as the latter and former rain unto the earth" (Ho 6:3).

"We must have revival," wrote Dr. Beecher. "It must rain faster, or we perish with drought."

REVIVE THY WORK, O LORD!

Revive Thy work, O Lord!
   Thy mighty arm make bare;
Speak with the voice that wakes the dead,
   And make Thy people hear!

Revive Thy work, O Lord!
   Disturb this sleep of death;
Quicken the smould'ring embers now
   By Thine Almighty breath.

Revive Thy work, O Lord!
   Create soul-thirst for Thee;
And hung'ring for the bread of life,
   Oh, may our spirits be!

Revive Thy work, O Lord!
   Exalt Thy precious name;
And by the Holy Ghost, our love
   For Thee and Thine inflame.

   Revive Thy work, O Lord,
   While here to Thee we bow;
   Descend, O gracious Lord, descend,
   O, come and bless us now!

FANNY J. CROSBY

12

THE PICTURE OF REVIVAL

Then said He unto me, Prophesy unto the wind, prophesy, son of man, and say to the wind, Thus saith the Lord God; Come from the four winds, O breath, and breathe upon these slain, that they may live.

So I prophesied as He commanded me, and the Breath came into them, and they lived, and stood up upon their feet, an exceeding great army. EZEKIEL 37:9-10.

"MAN'S EXTREMITY is God's opportunity." Although well worn, this succinct sentence is the message of Ezekiel chapter 37, to the twentieth-century church. It is just when God's people are saying to themselves, "Our bones are dried, and our hope is lost: we are cut off for our parts" (Eze 37:11) that God steps into the picture and gloriously demonstrates what He can do for a dispirited, defeated, and despairing people (Eze 37:11-14).

To dispel our deep-seated pessimism and to gain fresh hope, let us consider this chapter as containing God's answer to the church's present dilemma.

Without doubt, the key to the whole chapter is found in verses nine and ten. In verse nine, we have a most remarkable prayer, a divinely dictated prayer, a prayer that was immediately and exactly answered. "Come from the four winds, O breath, and breathe upon these slain, that they may live."

Now let us ask ourselves, Why was Ezekiel commanded

to invoke the advent and activity of the breath of heaven? Why was he instructed to invite the presence of the Spirit of God? These questions are best answered by a careful consideration of the results of the Spirit's coming.

Turning to verse ten we read, "The breath came into them, and they lived, and stood up upon their feet, an exceeding great army." As a direct result of the Spirit's intervention, there was LIFE—*"they lived";* there was POWER—*"they stood up upon their feet";* and there was UNITY—*"an exceeding great army." Life, power,* and *unity*—and, if you please, in that order.

Right here is supplied the reason we need the breath of heaven today. We need Him as the Spirit of life; we need Him as the Spirit of power, and we need Him as the Spirit of unity. He, and He alone, is God's answer to the church's dilemma today.

THE SPIRIT OF LIFE

We need, we desperately need, the breath of heaven as the Spirit of life.

Picture the scene of Ezekiel 37. By a supernatural transportation, the prophet finds himself in the midst of a valley of dry bones. All round him as far as eye can see lie dry bones, picked clean by birds of prey and bleached white by the hot Eastern sun. This is a scene of disaster and death.

As Ezekiel surveys the valley, filled with these ghastly remains of mortality, the Lord asks him a surprising question, "Son of man, can these bones live?" (37:3).

Amazed at such an inquiry, the prophet can only respond, "O LORD GOD, thou knowest." Then the prophet receives an equally surprising command, "Prophesy upon these bones, and say unto them, O ye dry bones, hear the word of the Lord" (37:4).

Ezekiel obeys and prophesies, and as he does so, he hears a strange, eerie sound, a shaking in the valley; and before him he sees the bones, once lying scattered and lifeless, begin to come together, one by one, until they form complete skeletons. And then before his wondering eyes, flesh and sinews come upon the skeletons, covering the bare bones; finally, skin covers the flesh.

However, although the bones have come together and although there are flesh and skin now covering the bones, there is—and Ezekiel emphasizes it—no breath in them. There is no life-giving principle operating in the corpses; there is no spirit to animate the dead bodies.

The words of verse nine, therefore, form the next step in the quickening of these skeletons. Ezekiel is commanded to pray to the breath of heaven, and as he obeys, we read, "The breath came into them, and they lived" (37:10). They lived! Without the breath of heaven, they had no life; with the breath of heaven, they lived.

The breath of heaven, then, is the Spirit of life; and it is only through His advent and activity that there is life in any realm—the physical, the spiritual, or the ecclesiastical.

Now, while this chapter is undoubtedly speaking first and foremost concerning the nation of Israel, by way of analogy we may apply the principles here taught to the plight and predicament of God's people today.

He is *spirit*ually dead who does not have the Spirit of life. When man was created, he possessed the life of God. When Adam transgressed, he lost the life of God and became spiritually dead, as dead as any of the skeletons in the valley of vision. The natural man, the Scriptures teach, is dead in sins and trespasses (Eph 2:1). "Dead in sins" can be written over every child of Adam's race.

The sinner's basic need, therefore, is to be quickened into life by the breath of heaven. He may be educated yet not have the Spirit of life. He may be moral yet not have the Spirit of life. He may be religious yet not have the Spirit of life. Indeed, he may even be fundamental yet not have the Spirit of life. Thus the Bible doctrine of man—so unpalatable

131

to modern humanity—is that he stands in need of the Spirit of life. Without the ministry of the breath of heaven, the world remains a vast graveyard, without a resurrection to be experienced or evidenced.

When a sinner comes to God in repentance and faith and is born again ("born from above," Jn 3:3, Zondervan ed. marg.), he receives the Spirit of life. Paul designates the breath of heaven as "the Spirit of life in Christ Jesus" (Ro 8:2). In various passages, the apostle speaks of the intervention of the Spirit of life (1 Co 2:14-15); the incoming of the Spirit of life (1 Co 2:12; Gal 3:2); the indwelling of the Spirit of life (1 Co 3:16); the inworking of the Spirit of life (Phil 1:6); and the infilling of the Spirit of life (Eph 5:18). Always he builds upon the unchanging and unchangeable fact that every believer in Christ Jesus has received the breath of heaven as the Spirit of life. The Spirit of life is the birthright of every child of God. In the light of the New Testament teaching concerning the Holy Spirit, there never can be doubt about this fact.

And yet, too often believers are content to be born again but not to enjoy and experience the fullness of the Spirit of life in Christ Jesus. Technically and theologically, every believer has the Spirit of life, but practically and experientially, many a believer knows little of the life of the Spirit. We need to recall that birth from heaven brings the breath of heaven. And He who came to give us life more abundant craves that we know something more of the Spirit of life.

The church of Jesus Christ, according to the New Testament, is formed of all believers in whom the Spirit of life is resident. There is always a danger in speaking of the church in the abstract because we may ignore or forget our individual responsibility as believers to be filled with the breath of heaven. The church is one body, but each member of that body is responsible to have in abundant measure the life of the Spirit.

132

In 1 Corinthians, Paul seems to indicate this twofold truth. In chapter 3, he speaks of believers collectively as being the "temple of God." In chapter 6, he speaks of the believers individually as being likewise the "temple of God." It is only as each Christian individually is filled with the Spirit of life that the church in turn is filled with the Spirit of life. As we remember this, we honor our own individual responsibility to be filled with the Spirit.

> O Breath of Life, come sweeping through us;
> Revive Thy Church with life and power.
> O Breath of Life, come cleanse, renew us,
> And fit Thy Church to meet this hour.

BESSIE PORTER HEAD

THE SPIRIT OF POWER

The breath of heaven is the Spirit of life. He is also the Spirit of power. The corpses not only lived, but they stood up upon their feet. They not only possessed the Spirit of life, the Spirit of life possessed them, and that life was evidenced as they stood up upon their feet.

Let us face the truth together. We who are evangelical profess to have received the Spirit of life. We maintain, on the authority of the Word of God, that each believer has been born again of God the Holy Spirit.

But, really, how much do we know of the Spirit of life as the Spirit of power? We know all about the doctrine of the Spirit, but how much do we know of the dynamic of the Spirit? We speak of the depths of Christian experience, but we live in the shallows. We are precise in our formulation of divine truth, but we are powerless to stem the advance of the enemy as he attacks the Christian church. We are fundamental, but to our shame, we must say that we are also feeble.

Only once let us see the relationship that exists between the Spirit and power; then we too will not only live but also will stand up upon our feet. The church needs to come to attention, to stand up, to become a power and a force in a world of chaos and crisis.

The relationship that exists between the Spirit and power is clearly taught in the Scriptures. Hear the testimony of Micah: "But truly I am full of power by the Spirit of the Lord" (Mic 3:8). See it in the life of the Lord Jesus: "God anointed Jesus of Nazareth with the Holy Ghost and with power" (Ac 10:38). Listen to the promise of the risen Lord: "Ye shall receive power, after that the Holy Ghost is come upon you" (Ac 1:8). Watch the life of Stephen: "Stephen, full of faith and power, did great wonders and miracles among the people" (Ac 6:8).

In the Acts of the Apostles, chapter 3, we are provided with a graphic illustration of the relationship between the Holy Spirit and power. The story is familiar to us all. "A certain man lame from his mother's womb," we are told, "was laid daily at the gate of the temple which is called Beautiful, to ask alms of them that entered into the temple."

When Peter spoke the authoritative word of command, he took the poor fellow by the right hand and lifted him up. Immediately his feet and ankle bones received strength. "And he leaping up stood, and walked, and entered with them into the temple, walking, and leaping, and praising God" (3:8).

Life the poor man had; power was his need. He was helpless and hopeless—and he had been that way from birth! But what a transformation is seen when God intervenes! And do we err if we see in his case a parable of many a believer—lame since birth, powerless to do exploits for God, totally dependent on others for a living? But there is hope! "In the name of Jesus Christ of Nazareth, rise up and walk!" (3:6) And He who is the Spirit of power as well as life will insure that such believers will be transformed into strong, sturdy children of God.

Breath of Calvary! Breath of Calvary!
Let us feel Thy quick'ning pow'r,
Cleansing, energizing, filling,
Every moment, every hour.

HERBERT TOVY

Used by permission of
Eva M. Tovy

THE SPIRIT OF UNITY

The breath of heaven is the Spirit of life, the Spirit of power, and He is also the *Spirit of unity.*

The order is divine. It is as we know Him as the Spirit of life that we are led to experience Him as the Spirit of power. And it is as we know Him both as the Spirit of life and the Spirit of Power that we come to know Him as the Spirit of unity.

We sing, "Like a mighty army moves the Church of God," but what a travesty of the truth! If ever the church of God is to be "terrible as an army with banners," if she is to be in truth "an exceeding great army," she will need the heavenly baptism of the breath of heaven.

We need the breath of heaven as the Spirit of unity because of present-day trends towards outward, organizational unity in Christendom.

We are told by some that the major problem of the church today is her lack of unity. Bring the divided denominations together, we are assured, and the millennium will be ushered in!

But, we ask, does the church need the kind of unity that has headquarters in Washington or in Rome? Is not the unity we need the unity that exists among men and women in whom the Spirit of God is resident, reigning, and operative? The bond of the Spirit comes only from the birth of the Spirit. The unity we seek, therefore, is the unity of men and women regenerate and infilled by the breath of heaven.

135

If ecumenically minded leaders are urging denominations to unite organizationally, it is high time that evangelically minded believers begin to demonstrate their true unity by closing up the ranks and by standing shoulder to shoulder in the army of the Lord. While we fear—and rightly so—any movement toward unity at the expense of the very fundamentals of the gospel, we should at the same time fear any division or schism that will further weaken the advance and spread of the gospel throughout the world. There is a unity to be kept, says Paul, and as believers, we need to press forward to that goal (Eph 4:3-6, 13).

Moreover, we need the breath of heaven as the Spirit of unity because of the sad divisions that do exist in the ranks of the Christian church. We cannot ignore the fact that fleshly and selfish men, seeking a following of their own, do cause divisions in the church. That is the clear teaching of 1 Corinthians 3:3. All too often believers come to blows over minor matters, fighting major battles over minor issues.

The day before the Battle of Trafalgar, Lord Nelson discovered that two of his officers, Collingwood and Rotherham, were not on speaking terms. Calling them together, he pointed to the enemy fleet and said, "Yonder, gentlemen, is the enemy. Now shake hands, and be friends."

Would that we could take the hands of some of our feuding fundamentalists and, indicating the true enemy, ask them to shake hands and be friends. How we need the breath of heaven to heal some of the divisions that exist among us!

Finally, we need the breath of heaven as the Spirit of unity in order to do the work that has been committed to us, namely, the task of world evangelization.

Study the church militant in the Acts of the Apostles. Out from that upper room where the early Christians had received their holy, heavenly baptism came that small but mighty army. Forth it came, flaming and burning, to set the world on fire, to conquer every foe, and to plant the banner of the cross in the very heart of the Roman empire before the record closes.

How did the early church accomplish so much by so few in so short a time? She had received the breath from heaven as the Spirit of life, the Spirit of power, and preeminently, as the Spirit of unity.

In the pioneering days of the Canadian West, a family was making its way by foot to a farmhouse, located several miles outside a prairie town. It was bitterly cold, and to make better time, the father and mother and their boy cut across a field of wheat that, because of the early snowfall, had not been harvested. For some reason, the boy became separated from his parents. After a fruitless search the parents decided to return to the village to enlist the help of as many of the local people as possible.

Nearly all the adults of the village turned out and began to search the field. After some time when no trace of the boy could be found, one of the searchers suggested that they all join hands and advance across the field, systematically searching the ground. Quickly the people joined hands and marched across the field. After just a few minutes, the call went out, "I've found him!" The boy had been found, but it was too late; he had succumbed to the bitter cold, and his life had been snuffed out.

As the father gazed upon the body of his son, he was overheard to say, "Oh, that we had joined hands sooner!" And when we stand at the judgment seat of Christ to receive the reward for the things done in the body, will not one of our regrets be that we had not joined hands sooner?

But wait. Here we are in a world where all around us men and women are dying without hope and without God. There is still time to save multitudes of these. Then, in Jesus' name let us join hands, let us march forth as an exceeding great army to "rescue the perishing, care for the dying." We have sung about it long enough; now then, let us join hands!

INTO THE DEPTHS WITH GOD

Like the wondrous river of the prophet's vision,
So the Holy Spirit floweth full and free,
Larger, deeper, fuller, still the river groweth,
Till it reach the fullness of the Crystal Sea.

Waters to the ankles, lo! the river deepens,
And we bathe our steppings in the holy flood.
Walking in the Spirit, stepping in His footprints,
Living on obedience, walking with our God.

Waters to the knees, O blessed Holy Spirit,
Teach our helpless hearts the wondrous power of prayer;
Breathe Thy prayer within us, waft it up to Heaven,
Help us like our Master, others' burdens bear.

Waters to the loins, we've reached the mighty river,
'Tis the promised filling of the Holy Ghost.
Plunge into the torrent, let it bear us onward
Till our lives repeat the Day of Pentecost.

Waters overhead, O blessing vast and boundless!
Spirit without measure, flowing full and free!
Let us know Thy fullness, pour the floods upon us,
Till we lose ourselves, and all our life in Thee.

Bright and beauteous river, on its banks are growing
Trees of bounteous verdure, fruits so rich and rare;
Leaves of life and healing, every joy and blessing—
All the founts of love and paradise are there.

J. OSWALD SANDERS
Used by permission

138

13

THE PLENITUDE OF REVIVAL

Afterward he brought me again unto the door of the house; and, behold, waters issued out from under the threshold of the house eastward: for the forefront of the house stood toward the east, and the waters came down from under from the right side of the house, at the south side of the altar.

And it shall come to pass, that every thing that liveth, which moveth, whithersoever the rivers shall come, shall live: and there shall be a very great multitude of fish, because these waters shall come thither: for they shall be healed; and every thing shall live whither the river cometh. EZEKIEL 47:1, 9

"I LOVE RIVERS," wrote Victor Hugo, and when the believer turns to the Scriptures, he, too, falls in love with rivers, the rivers of the Bible. We think of the Nile, "Heaven sent," as Homer described it; of the mighty Euphrates, on whose banks proud Babylon was built; and of the Jordan, small but significant river of God's chosen land. These are rivers that fascinate and charm.

But it is Ezekiel's mystic river, traced for us in Ezekiel 47:1-12, that intrigues and instructs us most. In this study we offer no novel interpretation. We propose to take it as a striking and suggestive symbol of "the fulness of the blessing of the gospel of Christ" (Ro 15:29) and as a divinely inspired commentary on the words of Psalm 46:4, "There is a river, the streams whereof shall make glad the city of God." No other figure employed in the Bible—and there are many of them—captures the essence of the life of victory in Christ as does a river, and in Ezekiel 47, that figure is worked out in wonderful detail.

In what ways, then, does this marvelous river symbolize the life that is available to us through the supply of the Spirit?

Let us think of three aspects of that life as symbolized by this river.

ITS ORIGIN

Let us be clear first as to the origin of this mighty river of blessing.

In his book, *The White Nile,* Alan Moorehead told how, for at least two thousand years, the mystery of the sources of the Nile was debated without an adequate answer being given. He wrote, "In these deserts [of Egypt] the river was life itself. Had it failed to flow, even for one season, then all Egypt perished. Not to know where the stream came from, not to have any sort of guarantee that it would continue—this was to live in a state of insecurity where only fatalism or superstition could reassure the mind."[1]

"Not to know where the stream came from"—that was the problem; but when we investigate Ezekiel's river, there is no secret, for he tells us,

> Afterward he brought me again unto the door of the huose; and, behold, waters issued out from under the threshold of the house eastward: for the forefront of the house stood toward the east, and the waters came down from under from the right side of the house, at the south side of the altar. Then brought he me out of the way of the gate northward, and led me about the way without unto the utter gate by the way that looketh eastward; and, behold, there ran out waters on the right side."

Surely this revelation of the river's origin fortifies faith and vanquishes fatalism!

Let us look at Ezekiel's explanation in some detail.

When Ezekiel refers to the house, he is, of course, alluding to the temple which he had already been shown in his vision. The account of this vision occupies the last main section of the book of Ezekiel, that is chapters 40-48.

While it is our conviction that this remarkable vision will have a fulfillment in relation to Israel during the millennial kingdom, we believe that it is possible to apply the underlying principles to us today. According to Paul in 2 Corinthians 6:16, believers today are "the temple of the living God."

We call attention, therefore, to two aspects of the origin of this river, symbol of the abundant life in Christ.

First, the waters of this river had their origin generally in the temple of God. Ezekiel tells us that the "waters issued out from under the threshold of the house."

Here is a most profitable insight into the origin of this river.

The temple is, first, typical of the life that is built according to the plan of God. The temple of Ezekiel 40-48 is constructed according to the divine blueprint.

In Ezekiel 43:11, the prophet is commanded to show to the exiles in Babylonia "the form of the house, and the fashion thereof, and the goings out thereof, and the comings in thereof, and all the forms thereof, and all the ordinances thereof, and all the forms thereof, and all the laws thereof." This was to demonstrate to the people of Israel that God had a plan already drawn up for them and for their new temple.

In the same way, the Scriptures reveal that God has a plan for each of His children, and it is the life built according to that plan that enjoys the life more abundant.

In examining our hearts, we must ask ourselves such questions as these: Have I realized that God has a plan for my life as exact and as particular as that for the temple of Ezekiel 40-48? Have I acknowledged that He has a blueprint for every area and aspect of my life—spiritual, social, domestic, personal?

God's plan is all-inclusive, and when we build according to His plan, then we experience the fullness of His blessing.

But we may go a step further. The temple is also typical of the life that is blessed with the presence of God.

Two scenes presented to us in the book of Ezekiel drive home this point.

In Ezekiel 8-11, we have the removal of the glory of the Lord from the temple at Jerusalem. This took place historically when Jerusalem with its precious pearl, the temple, was abandoned by Jehovah to the Babylonians. Thus in 11:23 we read, "The glory of the LORD went up from the midst of the city, and stood upon the mountain which is on the east side of the city."

But in Ezekiel 43:1-6, the action is reversed. Here we have the return of the glory of the Lord to the restored temple. "The glory of the LORD came into the house by the way of the gate whose prospect is toward the east. . . . and, behold, the glory of the LORD filled the house" (43:4-5).

It is from this glory-filled house that God's river of life flows.

According to Peter, our lives should be glory filled. Listen to him as he writes to Christian believers. He refers to the Lord Jesus Christ, and states, "Whom having not seen, ye love; in whom, though now ye see him not, yet believing, ye rejoice with joy unspeakable and full of glory" (1 Pe 1:8).

"The glory of the LORD filled the house." "Ye rejoice with joy . . . full of glory." Is that our experience? It may be, and by God's grace it shall be!

There is a third aspect that should be mentioned. The temple is also typical of the life that is beautified with the purity of God. In Ezekiel 43:12, we have the law of the house. "This is the law of the house; Upon the top of the mountain the whole limit thereof round about shall be most holy. Behold, this is the law of the house."

That means purity! Holiness unto the Lord! The person who possesses the river of life is set apart for God's glory and for God's service. "O worship the LORD in the beauty of holiness" (Ps 96:9).

In summary, then, God's river of life has its origin in the temple, and that temple may be taken as typical of the life that is characterized by the plan, the presence, and the purity of God.

But we may trace the origin of this river not only in general terms but also in specific terms. Ezekiel tells us, "The waters came down from under from the right side of the house, at the south side of the altar." Here the origin of the river is pinpointed in terms of direction, "the right side of the house, at the south side of the altar."

That there seems to be a definite relation between the house itself and the altar is made clear by Ezekiel's description. The river emerges from under the threshold of the house, but in its early stages, it flows by the altar of burnt offering.

Is this not designed to teach us that it is the life that knows practically and personally the meaning of Christ's cross that comes into the experience of the river of life? When John sees "a pure river of water of life, clear as crystal," he sees it "proceeding out of the throne of God and of the Lamb" (Rev 22:1).

God's river of life comes to us through the atonement of the Lamb of God. It is vitally and eternally linked to the redemption accomplished by the sacrificial Sufferer on Calvary.

There is a fable to the effect that at the spot where a great military hero fell in death, a perennial spring started, gushing forth in abundance. At Calvary there was opened a spring of life-giving water that flows on full and free. Our great

Captain laid down His life, and out of that death there comes life to us. Only as our lives are vitally linked to that death can we know the fullness of His risen life in us and through us.

ITS OUTFLOWING

We have traced the origin of God's river of life. Look now at Ezekiel's description of its outflowing.

> When the man that had the line in his hand went forth eastward, he measured a thousand cubits, and he brought me through the waters; the waters were to the ankles. Again he measured a thousand, and brought me through the waters; the waters were to the knees. Again he measured a thousand, and brought me through; the waters were to the loins. Afterward he measured a thousand; and it was a river that I could not pass over: for the waters were risen, waters to swim in, a river that could not be passed over" (47:3-5).

Let us consider some striking features of Ezekiel's river. There is, for example, the mystery of this river of life. Here is a river that rises within the temple of the Lord, built on Mount Zion, and yet without any tributaries augmenting its flow; it becomes deeper and deeper as it pours forward and onward. We are told that the source of the Amazon is in or near Lake Ninococha, sixteen-thousand feet up in the Andes Mountains. But the Amazon is fed by countless tributaries.

There is no way, therefore, to avoid the use of the word *mystery*. And as we relate the word mystery to this river of life, we do well to relate it, in addition, to Christian experience. There is a mystery about Christian life and experience that cannot be explained. In these days when conversion is being psychologically analyzed and clinically documented, let us remember that there are aspects of Christian experience that cannot be examined or explained. "The wind bloweth where it listeth," said the Lord Jesus to Nicodemus, "and thou hearest the sound thereof, but canst not tell whence it cometh, and whither it goeth: so is every one that is born of the spirit" (Jn 3:8).

All movements born of God partake of the mysterious. We must be prepared to say with the hymn writer,

> I know not how the Spirit moves,
> Convincing men of sin;
> Revealing Jesus through the Word,
> Creating faith within.

> DANIEL W. WHITTLE

That leads us to stress the miracle of the outflowing of this river. This river is the product of God's creative power. It reveals that God is at work on behalf of His people.

Let us not be afraid of that word *supernatural*. Christian experience cannot be explained in terms of the natural. According to Paul, "It is God which worketh in you both to will and to do of His good pleasure" (Phil 2:13). Let us preserve the emphasis upon the supernatural aspect of Christian life and experience. We are not offering men and women "natural religion," but supernatural life from God.

Finally, we note the measure of this river of life. First, the waters were to the ankles; then, to the knees; then, to the loins; and finally, they were waters to swim in, a river that could not be passed over. Such is the measure of the river.

We are sure that there are various applications possible for this aspect of the river. For example, are we not taught thereby that our Christian life and experience is progressive? We set out, hesitantly at first, perhaps, into the life of God's fullness; soon we find that it has increased to our knees and then to our loins. Finally, we discover that the waters form a river to swim in, so strong and steady is the flow of divine life.

145

We have traced the origin of God's river of life to the temple. We have followed Ezekiel as he saw the outflowing of this wonderful river. Our final consideration relates to the outcome of this river. Here again the prophet describes this aspect for us.

> He said unto me, Son of man, hast thou seen this? Then he brought me, and caused me to return to the brink of the river. Now when I had returned, behold, at the bank of the river were very many trees on the one side and on the other.
>
> Then said he unto me. These waters issue out toward the east country, and go down into the desert, and go into the sea: which being brought forth into the sea, the waters shall be healed. And it shall come to pass, that every thing that liveth, which moveth, whithersoever the rivers shall come, shall live: and there shall be a very great multitude of fish, because these waters shall come thither: for they shall be healed; and every thing shall live whither the river cometh.
>
> And it shall come to pass, that the fishers shall stand upon it from En-gedi even unto En-eglaim; they shall be a place to spread forth nets; their fish shall be according to their kinds, as the fish of the great sea, exceeding many. But the miry places thereof and the marishes thereof shall not be healed; they shall be given to salt.
>
> And by the river upon the bank thereof, on this side and on that side, shall grow all trees for meat, whose leaf shall not fade, neither shall the fruit thereof be consumed: it shall bring forth new fruit according to his months, because their waters they issued out of the sanctuary: and the fruit thereof shall be for meat, and the leaf thereof for medicine (47:6-12).

Here are four blessed and beneficial results of this river.

First, there is life where there was once death. "Every thing shall live whither the river cometh." Down into the Dead Sea flows that river of life, and the noxious waters of that lifeless lake are regenerated. It is a river that counteracts death.

How much we need this river of life in our society today. Only God can bring life into dead churches. We are in danger of looking for other schemes and programs to bring life, but we must shun these and look to the God of life.

Second, there is healing where there was once sickness. "The waters," we read, "shall be healed." It is instructive to note the language used here. Evidently it is the polluted waters that are under consideration. But the prophet is told that the waters shall be *healed,* not cleansed. The waters are for the health of those who drink. This is God's "fountain of youth," for which men have sought for centuries.

This is what is needed today. Society needs its sources of water healed. Its laws, its customs, its culture, its arts—all these need the healing influence of God's river of life. And it is from the church that these waters are to flow. We are to be as the waters of the Amazon that flow out for miles into the ocean and counteract the saltiness of the sea.

Third, there is success where there was once failure. "Their fish shall be according to their kinds, as the fish of the great sea, exceeding many." Where once fishermen caught no fish, now there shall be an abundance of the harvest of the sea. The river of life has come, and once again, "the waters bring forth abundantly" (Gen 1:20).

What a word is this for discouraged fishers of men! Oh, how many lives are marked and marred by failure; But let God's river of life come and failure is turned into success. Then will our net enclose "a great multitude of fishes" (Lk 5:6).

Finally, there is fruitfulness where once there was barrenness. "By the river upon the bank thereof, on this side and on that side, shall grow all trees for meat, whose leaf shall not fade, neither shall the fruit thereof be consumed: it shall bring forth new fruit according to his months, because their waters they issued out of the sanctuary: and the fruit thereof shall be for meat, and the leaf thereof for medicine."

Here surely is a parallel to the experience of the blessed

man of Psalm 1. "He shall be," says the psalmist, "like a tree planted by the rivers of water, that bringeth forth his fruit in his season; his leaf also shall not wither; and whatsoever he doeth shall prosper."

In Philippians 1:11, Paul exhorts us to be "filled with the fruits of righteousness, which are by Jesus Christ, unto the glory and praise of God." And this is made possible by the influence of God's river of life.

Life out of death! Health out of sickness! Success out of failure! Fruitfulness out of barrenness! This is the outcome of God's miracle river.

There is a Greek myth involving Hercules. As a punishment for his sin, Hercules was assigned twelve prodigious tasks to complete. One of these tasks was to clean the stables of Augeas, King of Elis. Augeas kept three-thousand oxen in them, and the stables had not been cleaned for thirty years. To top it all Hercules was commanded to clean them in one day! But Hercules was not discouraged. He simply turned the Alpheus and Peneus rivers into the stalls, and the force of the combined rivers cleaned the stables.

In its ministry of bringing cleansing and purity to men, has the church overlooked God's rivers of life? Are we looking to other methods and measures to accomplish the task, only to find that the task defeats us and discourages us? Let us turn back to the river of divine life and blessing and channel it into a polluted world. Then, and only then, will sin give way before holiness, unbelief before faith, and despair before hope.

In his poem, "To the River Charles," Henry W. Longfellow says, "Thou hast taught me, Silent River, many a lesson, deep and long." So our study of God's river of life has taught us many lessons to be applied to daily living. "Rivers are highways," said Blaise Pascal, and if we will make ourselves available to God, we can see His river of life become the highway of holiness for those around us.

NOTES

PREFACE

1. David Lazell, *From the Forest I Came,* p. 23.
2. *The Religious Reawakening in America,* ed. Joseph Newman, p. 11.
3. See, for example, K. Neill Foster, *Revolution of Love;* Bernard and Marjorie Palmer, *The Winds of God Are Blowing;* Freda Teichrob, *His Touch;* Charles R. Tarr, *A New Wind Blowing!* One Divine Moment, ed. Robert E. Coleman; Kurt Koch, *The Revival in Indonesia, Revival Fires in Canada, Victory Through Persecution;* Patricia St. John, *Breath of Life.*
4. John Thomas, foreword to *Cataracts of Revival,* by G. J. Morgan (London: Marshall, Morgan & Scott, n.d.), pp. 5, 6.

CHAPTER 1

1. Ernest M. Wadsworth, *Will Revival Come?* (Chicago: Moody, n. d.), pp. 12, 13.
2. John Shearer, *Old Time Revivals* (London: Pickering & Inglis, 1929), p. 23.
3. R. B. Jones, *Rent Heavens* (London: Pioneer Mission, 1948), p. 88.
4. J. Edwin Orr, *The Church Must First Repent* (London: Marshall, Morgan, & Scott, n. d.), pp. 17, 18.
5. D. M. Panton, clipping from cover of *The Dawn Magazine.*
6. Frank G. Beardsley, *A History of American Revivals* (New York: American Tract Soc., 1904), p. 215.
7. Leonard Ravenhill, *Why Revival Tarries,* pp. 136-37.
8. Charles G. Finney, *Revivals of Religion* (London: Marshall, Morgan, & Scott, 1913), p. 28.
9. Ibid., pp. 28, 29, W. H. Harding's footnote.
10. G. W. Hervey, *Manual of Revivals* (New York: Funk & Wagnalls, 1884), p. XXVI.
11. Jonathan Edwards, *The Narrative,* p. 93.
12. David Matthews, *I Saw the Welsh Revival* (Chicago: Moody, 1951), p. 121.
13. Duncan Campbell, *The Lewis Awakening* (Edinburgh: Faith Mission, 1954), p. 29.
14. Ibid.
15. James Burns, *Revivals: Their Laws and Leaders* (Grand Rapids: Baker, 1960), pp. 40, 41.

16. Ibid., p. 41.
17. Robert W. Dale as quoted in ibid., p. 43.
18. J. Edwin Orr, *The Second Evangelical Awakening in Britain*, p. 263.
19. C. E. Autrey, *Revivals of the Old Testament* (Grand Rapids: Zondervan, 1960), p. 24-25.
20. Alan Redpath in Ravenhill, p. 42.
21. Quoted by W. B. Knight, *3000 Illustrations for Christian Service* (Grand Rapids: Eerdmans, 1957), p. 566.

CHAPTER 2

1. Jonathan Goforth, *By My Spirit*, p. 135.

CHAPTER 3

1. John Wesley, quoted by Martin Wells Knapp, *Revival Kindlings* (Albion, Mich.: The Revivalist, 1890), p. 259.
2. Leonard Ravenhill, *Revival Praying*, p. 176.

CHAPTER 5

1. R. B. Jones, *Rent Heavens*, p. 22.
2. Ibid., p. 41.
3. J. Burns, *Revivals: Their Laws and Leaders*, p. 30.
4. J. D. Drysdale, *The Price of Revival* (London: Oliphants, n. d.), p. 32.
5. James McQuilkin, quoted by J. Edwin Orr, *The Second Evangelical Awakening in Britain*, p. 39.
6. Adam Clarke, quoted by Thomas Payne, *Revivals: How Promoted* (London: Marshall, Morgan, & Scott, n. d.), p. 133.
7. J. D. Drysdale, *Prophet of Holiness*, ed. Norman Grubb (Woking, Eng.: Lutterworth, 1955), p. 119.
8. Bishop Hopkins, quoted by William P. Pearce, *The Revival Thermometer* (Dayton: United Brethren Publ., 1905), p. 112.

CHAPTER 6

1. W. A. McKay, *Outpourings of the Spirit* (Philadelphia: Presbyterian Board of Publ., 1890), p. 10.
2. Norman Grubb, *Continuous Revival*, p. 7.

CHAPTER 7

1. G. W. Hervey, *Manual of Revivals*, p. 3.
2. C. G. Finney, *Lectures on Revivals of Religions* (Old Tappan, N. J.: Revell, n. d.), p. 49.
3. W. B. Pearce, *The Revival Thermometer* (Atlanta, Ga.: United Brethren Publ., 1905), p. 27.
4. C. E. Autrey, *Revivals of the Old Testament*, p. 24.
5. Theodore Bamber, *Preparing the Way* (Atlantic City: World Wide Revival Prayer Movement, 1941), p. 22.
6. DeWitt Talmage, quoted by Thomas Payne, *Apostolic Christianity* (London: S. J. Fraser, n. d.), pp. 60-61.
7. D. Matthews, *I Saw the Welsh Revival*, p. 9.
8. Alexander Whyte, quoted by John T. Carson, *God's River in Spate* (Belfast: Publ. Board, Presbyterian Church in Ireland, 1928), p. 126.
9. D. Campbell, *God's Standard* (Fort Washington: Christian Lit. Crusade, 1967), p. 58.
10. H. P. Barker, *Windows in Words* (London: Pickering & Inglis, 1954), p. 130.

Chapter 8

1. N. Grubb, *Continuous Revival,* p. 13.
2. Quoted by J. D. Drysdale, *The Price of Revival,* p. 96.
3. George Cokeyn, "Preface to the Reader," introducing "The Acceptable Sacrifice," in *The Entire Works of John Bunyan,* ed. Henry Stebbing (Toronto: Virtue, Yorston, n.d.), 3:335.
4. Ibid., p. 40.
5. A. Douglas Brown, *Revival Addresses* (London: Marshall, Morgan, & Scott, 1922), p. 80-82. Used by permission of the publisher.
6. John Bunyan, *Entire Works of John Bunyan,* 3:359.

Chapter 10

1. Samuel Clark, *Holy Bible with Commentary,* ed. F. C. Cook (London: John Murray, 1871), 1:540.
2. Oswald Allis, *New Bible Commentary,* ed. F. Davidson, A. M. Stibbs, and E. F. Kevan (Grand Rapids: Eerdmans, 1953), p. 143.
3. George Williams, *The Student's Commentary* (London: Oliphants, 1949), p. 70.

Chapter 11

1. A. B. Simpson, *The Land of Promise* (Harrisburg, Pa.: Christian Publ., 1969), p. 52.

Chapter 13

1. Alan Moorehead, *The White Nile* (New York: Dell, 1960), p. 60.

151

BIBLIOGRAPHY

THE FOLLOWING BIBLIOGRAPHY includes books of sermons on revival, biographies of outstanding leaders in revival, and histories of revival. The books, all of which are still in print at this writing, represent both evangelical and secular interpretations of the meaning of revival. Unfortunately, few evangelical writers have studied the history of revival in depth; thus we are dependent in measure upon the works of nonevangelical writers for source material relating to the history of revival, especially revival in North America.

Allen, W. E. *The History of Revivals of Religion*. Belfast: Revival Pub. 1951. A short introduction to the revivals of the past.

America's Great Revivals. Minneapolis: Bethany Fellowship, n.d. This little book contains chapters originally appearing as articles in *Christian Life* magazine.

Appelman, Hyman. *Revival Sermons*. Grand Rapids: Baker, 1966. Sermons on revival by one of America's great evangelists.

———. *Sermons on the Holy Spirit*. Grand Rapids: Baker, 1962. These sermons emphasize the work of the Holy Spirit in revival and evangelism.

Beaurepaire, Anthony. *George Whitefield and the Great Evangelical Awakening*. London: Protestant Truth Soc., 1972. A brief introduction to Whitefield and his ministry.

Boles, John B. *The Great Revival, 1787-1805*. Lexington: U. Press of Kentucky, 1972. An attempt to determine "the origins of the Southern evangelical mind."

Bumsted, J. M. *The Great Awakening*. Waltham, Mass.: Blaisdell, 1970. Subtitled *The Beginnings of Evangelical Pietism in America*.

Bushman, Richard L., ed. *The Great Awakening.* New York: Atheneum, 1970. A collection of documents on the revival of religion, 1740-1745, published for the Institute of Early American History and Culture at Williamsburg, Virginia.

Cairns, Earle E. *The Christian in Society.* Chicago: Moody, 1973. A revised edition of *Saints and Society,* being an attempt to set forth principles for Christian involvement in society based upon the work and example of such men as Wilberforce and Howard.

Campbell, Duncan. *The Price and Power of Revival.* Fort Washington: Christian Lit. Crusade, 1962. Four heartwarming messages from the pen of the late Duncan Campbell, used of God in the revival that came to the islands of Lewis and Harris, 1949-53.

————. *God's Answer.* Fort Washington: Christian Lit. Crusade, 1967. More sermons on themes associated with revival.

————. *God's Standard.* Fort Washington: Christian Lit. Crusade, 1967. More sermons on themes associates with revival.

Cartwright, Peter. *Autobiography of Peter Cartwright.* Nashville: Abingdon, 1956. The remarkable story of a Methodist circuit rider who preached the gospel for fifty-three years (1803-1856).

Cleveland, C. C. *The Great Revival in the West, 1797-1805.* Gloucester, Mass.: Peter Smith, 1959. An introduction to the character and results of a US revival of religion.

Coleman, Robert E. *Dry Bones Can Live Again.* Old Tappan, N.J.: Revell, 1969. An excellent study manual on revival in the local church.

————, ed. *One Divine Moment.* Old Tappan, N.J.: Revell, 1970. The story of the 1970 revival on the campus of Asbury College and Asbury Theological Seminary.

Colton, Calvin. *History and Character of American Revivals of Religion.* New York: AMS, 1973. A reprint of the 1832 edition, which was written by Colton for British Christians to inform them concerning American revivals of religion.

Cowing, Cedric B. *The Great Awakening and the American Revolution: Colonial Thought in the 18th Century.* Chicago: Rand McNally, 1972. An attempt to show that the Great Awakening contributed to the American Revolution.

Cross, Whitney R. *The Burned-Over District.* New York: Harper

& Row, 1965. Subtitled *The Social and Intellectual History of Enthusiastic Religion in Western New York, 1800-1850.*

Davenport, F. Morgan. *Primitive Traits in Religious Revivals.* New York: Negro Universities Press, 1968. A reprint of a book first published by MacMillan in 1905, largely unsympathetic to revival.

Davies, W. E. *As Eagles Fly.* Hamilton: Bible Christian Union, 1971. A book containing a number of short, scriptural chapters on the general principles of revival.

Duncan, Homer, ed. *We Must Have Revival.* Lubbock: Missionary Crusader, n.d. A collection of articles by various authors on aspects of revival and revival leaders.

Edman, V. Raymond. *Finney Lives On: The Man, His Revival Methods, and His Message.* Minneapolis: Bethany Fellowship, 1971. An examination of the ministry of Charles G. Finney that seeks to apply the principles deduced therefrom to the church's present condition.

Edwards, Jonathan. *The Narrative.* W. Asheville: Revival Lit., n.d. An abridged version of Edwards' classic, with a biographical sketch, notes, and comments by James A. Stewart.

Evans, Eifion. *The Welsh Revival of 1904.* Port Talbot: Evangelical Movement of Wales, 1969. An excellent and sympathetic study of a twentieth-century revival.

Fawcett, Arthur. *The Cambuslang Revival.* London: Banner of Truth, 1971. An excellent presentation and evaluation of the Scottish evangelical revival of the eighteenth century.

Finney, Charles G. *C. G. Finney: An Autobiography.* New York: Revell, 1903. The life of the great evangelist.

———. *How to Promote a Revival.* Belfast: Revival Publ., n.d. Brief selections from Finney's larger work on revival.

———. *Power from on High.* London: Victory Press, 1971. A discussion of the meaning of the biblical phrase, "power from on high."

———. *Revival Fire.* Minneapolis: Bethany Fellowship, n.d. A collection of letters on revivals written by C. G. Finney to his friends, especially ministers of the gospel.

———. *Revival Lectures.* New York: Revell, n.d. Lectures that proceed on the basis that a "revival is as naturally a result of

154

the use of appropriate means as a crop is of the use of its appropriate means."

————. *Revival Truths.* Belfast: Revival Publ., n.d. Short chapters taken from Finney's larger work on revival.

————. *Short Life of Charles G. Finney by Himself.* Belfast: Revival Publ., n.d. A brief introduction to the life of the great evangelist.

Fischer, Harold A. *Reviving Revivals.* Springfield: Gospel Publ., 1950. An attempt to show that Pentecostalism is in line with the great revivals of the past.

Foster, K. Neill. *Revolution of Love.* Minneapolis: Bethany Fellowship, Dimension Books, 1973. An account of the Canadian revival of 1971-72, its impetus and impact.

Gaustad, Edwin S. *The Great Awakening in New England.* Chicago: Quadrangle, 1968. A historian looks at the Great Awakening of 1740.

Gewehr, Wesley M. *The Great Awakening in Virginia, 1740-1790.* Gloucester, Mass.: Peter Smith, 1965. A detailed study attempting to show the influence of the Great Awakening upon the various denominations in the South.

Goen, C. C. *Revivalism and Separatism in New England, 1740-1800.* Hamden, Conn.: Shoe String, 1969. A major interpretation of the eighteenth-century religious history of the U.S.

Goforth, Jonathan. *By My Spirit.* Minneapolis: Bethany Fellowship, 1964. Goforth's experiences with revival movements taking place in China, Korea, and Manchuria in the opening part of the twentieth century.

Goforth, Rosalind. *Goforth of China.* Minneapolis: Bethany Fellowship, n.d. The story of Jonathan Goforth, missionary-evangelist and exponent of revival.

Greenfield, John. *When the Spirit Came.* Minneapolis: Bethany Fellowship, 1967. Originally published as *Power from on High,* the story of the Moravian revival of 1727.

Grubb, Norman. *Continuous Revival.* Fort Washington: Christian Lit. Crusade, 1961. A quote from this book: "Revival is not so much a vertical outpouring from heaven, for the Reviver is already here in His temple, the bodies of the redeemed; it is more a horizontal outmoving of the Reviver through these temples into the world."

Heimert, Alan & Miller, Perry, eds. *The Great Awakening.* Indianapolis: Bobbs-Merrill, 1967. A collection of documents "illustrating the crisis and its consequences."

James, H. C. & Rader, Paul. *Halls Aflame.* Wilmore, Ky.: Asbury Theological Seminary, 1966. An exciting account of the spontaneous revivals at Asbury College in 1950 and 1958.

Keller, Charles Roy. *The Second Great Awakening in Connecticut.* Hamden, Conn.: Shoe String, 1968. A study of American religious revival at the turn of the nineteenth century.

Koch, Kurt. *Revival Fires in Canada.* Grand Rapids: Kregel, 1973. A sketchy account of the revival that began in parts of Canada in 1971; unfortunately contains a number of factual errors.

————. *The Revival in Indonesia.* Grand Rapids: Kregel, n.d. A detailed account of the recent religious awakening in Indonesia, aspects of which are still causing controversy.

————. *Victory Through Persecution.* Grand Rapids: Kregel, 1972. Published in Britain with the title, *The Korean Revival,* an account of spiritual awakening in the Korean church.

Lacy, Jr., Benjamin R. *Revivals in the Midst of the Years.* Nashville: Royal Publ. 1968. A focus upon the history of revivals, especially in the U.S., originally given as the Smyth Lectures at Columbia Theological Seminary.

Lazell, David. *From the Forest I Came.* Chicago: Moody, 1973. The fascinating story of Gipsy Smith, a great evangelist.

Lovejoy, D. S. *Religious Enthusiasm and the Great Awakening.* Englewood Cliffs, N.J.: Prentice-Hall, 1969. Historical materials that bear on the subject of "religious enthusiasm," and attempts to evaluate the character and consequences of this aspect of the Great Awakening.

Maxson, Charles H. *The Great Awakening in the Middle Colonies.* Gloucester, Mass.: Peter Smith, 1958. A detailed account of the Great Awakening in the Middle Colonies, including chapters on some of the leaders.

McCheyne, Robert Murray. *Robert M. M'Cheyne: Memoir and Remains.* London: Banner of Truth, 1966. The fullest account of one of Scotland's most godly preachers; including many of his sermons.

McLoughlin, Jr., William G. *Modern Revivalism.* New York: Ronald Press, 1959. The author traces the history of revivalism from C. G. Finney to Billy Graham.

————, ed. *The American Evangelicals, 1800-1900.* New York: Harper & Row, 1968. An anthology of writings by Evangelicals during the nineteenth century.

Mecklin, John M. *The Story of American Dissent.* Port Washington: Kennikat, 1970. Various materials relating to the influence of revivals on dissent.

Modersohn, Ernst. *Men of Revival in Germany.* Frankfurt/Main: Herold, n.d. An introduction to some leaders of revival in nineteenth-century Germany.

Newman, Joseph, ed. *The Religious Reawakening in America.* Washington, D.C.: U. S. News & World Report, 1972. An evaluation of various contemporary religious movements in North America.

Nissenbaum, Stephen, ed. *The Great Awakening at Yale College.* Belmont: Wadsworth, 1972. A collection of documents from the years, 1741-1745, recounting the story and influence of the great awakening at Yale.

Oakes, J. P. *Toward Revival.* Grand Rapids: Baker, 1966. A series of messages on revival.

Orr, J. Edwin. *Campus Aflame.* Glendale, Calif.: Gospel Light, 1971. A demonstration of the influence of revival among students upon Christianity.

————. *Evangelical Awakenings in India.* New Delhi: Christian Lit. Institute, 1970. The only available study on revival in India.

————. *The Fervent Prayer.* Chicago: Moody, 1974. A study of the worldwide impact of the Great Awakening of 1858. Second in a trilogy: the first, *The Flaming Tongue;* the third, *The Eager Feet,* a discussion of awakenings during the years 1790 to 1840, soon to be released.

————. *The Flaming Tongue.* Chicago: Moody, 1973. An excellent introduction to revivals in our century, including accounts of the Spirit's work in Britain, North America, Australia, and India.

————. *The Second Evangelical Awakening in Britain.* London: Marshall, Morgan & Scott, 1949. A thoroughly researched presentation of the nineteenth-century revival in Britain.

157

———. *The Light of the Nations*. Grand Rapids: Eerdmans, 1965. The story of evangelical renewal and advance in the nineteenth century.

Olford, Stephen. *Heart-Cry for Revival*. Grand Rapids: Zondervan, 1962. Eight expository messages, that define the characteristics, conditions, and consequences of revival.

Palmer, Bernard, and Palmer, Marjorie. *The Winds of God Are Blowing*. Wheaton: Tyndale, 1973. An introduction to various contemporary religious movements, some orthodox, some non-evangelical.

Peters, G. W. *Indonesia Revival: Focus on Timor*. Grand Rapids: Zondervan, 1973. A fully researched evaluation of the spiritual awakening in Indonesia.

Pollock, J. C. *George Whitefield and the Great Awakening*. New York: Doubleday, 1972.

Ravenhill, Leonard. *Meat for Men*. Zachary: Fires of Revival, 1973. A collection of short articles on revival.

———. *Revival Praying*. Zachary: Fires of Revival, 1973. Pungent chapters on a great theme.

———. *Sodom Had No Bible*. Zachary: Fires of Revival, 1971. Keen analysis of the church's plight, including portraits of ten revival preachers.

———. *Why Revival Tarries*. Zachary: Fires of Revival, 1973. Twenty short chapters on the general theme of revival.

Rutman, Darrett, B., ed. *The Great Awakening: Event and Exegesis*. New York: Kreiger, 1970. An introduction to and evaluation of the Great Awakening of the mideighteenth century.

Smith, Timothy L. *Revivalism & Social Reform*. New York: Harper & Row, 1965. A study by an evangelical author of American Protestantism on the eve of the Civil War.

Stearns, Monroe. *The Great Awakening, 1720-1760*. New York: Franklin Watts, 1970. An illustrated account of the Great Awakening subtitled *Religious Revival Rouses Americans' Sense of Individual Liberties*. Designed for young people.

Stewart, James A. *Invasion of Wales by the Spirit Through Evan Roberts*. Fort Washington: Christian Lit. Crusade, n.d. A sympathetic account of the revival in Wales, beginning in November 1904.

————. *Revival and the Church.* W. Asheville: Revival Lit., 1968. Formerly Part One of the book *Open Windows,* a collection of revival themes written by one who has been greatly used in the work of revival.

————. *Revival and You.* W. Asheville: Revival Lit., 1969. Formerly Part Two of the book *Open Windows.*

————. *Revival Behind the Iron Curtain.* W. Asheville, N.C.: Revival Lit., 1963. A brief account of revival scenes in Eastern European countries.

————. *William Chalmers Burns.* W. Asheville, N.C.: Revival Lit., 1964. A brief introduction to a contemporary and co-worker of Robert Murray McCheyne.

————. *Your Personal Revival.* W. Asheville, N.C.: Revival Lit., n.d. A brief challenge to appropriate God's power in revival.

Stewart, James A., and Stewart, Ruth. *The Wonder of God's Tomorrow.* W. Asheville, N.C.: Revival Lit., 1966. A collection of sermons on revival and associated themes.

St. John, Patricia. *Breath of Life.* London: Norfolk, 1971. A stirring account of what has been called the most enduring revival of modern times, including the beginnings of gospel work in Rwanda and Burundi.

Sweet, William W. *Revivalism in America.* Nashville: Abingdon, n.d. A study of the origin, growth, and influence of revivalism in North America.

Tarr, Charles R. *A New Wind Blowing.* Anderson: Warner, 1972. A pastor's account of the revival that came to his church in Anderson, Indiana, as a result of a visit of students from Asbury College.

Teichrob, Freda, ed. *His Touch.* Wyoming, Mich.: Paris, 1973. A collection of letters originating in the revival on the Canadian prairies, 1971-1972.

Torrey, R. A. *How to Find Fullness of Power in Christian Life and Service.* Minneapolis: Bethany Fellowship, n.d. A classic statement on the Spirit's fullness.

Tracy, Joseph. *The Great Awakening.* New York: Arno Press & New York Times, 1969. A book, first published in 1845, dealing with the history of the revival of religion in the time of Edwards and Whitefield.

159

Voke, Stanley, *Reality*. Fort Washington: Christian Lit. Crusade, 1964. A simply written booklet, a searching study of personal revival through discussion of brokenness, God's grace, and the way of peace.

Wallis, Arthur. *In the Day of Thy Power*. Fort Washington: Christian Lit. Crusade, 1956. A clear and comprehensive examination of the scriptural principles of revival.

Watt, Eva Stuart. *Dynamite in Europe*. W. Asheville: Revival Lit., 1962. The account of evangelistic meetings and revival in Eastern and Central Europe just before and just after the outbreak of World War II.

Weisberger, Bernard A. *They Gathered at the River*. Chicago: Quadrangle, 1966. Subtitled *The Story of the Great Revivalists and their Impact upon Religion in America,* including Beecher, Finney, and Moody.

Whitefield, George. *Whitefield's Journals*. London: Banner of Truth, 1965. The most complete collection of Whitefield's journals in print.

Wirt, Sherwood. *Jesus Power*. New York: Harper & Row, 1972. A fine study of the meaning of spiritual power.

Wood, A. Skevington. *And With Fire*. Fort Washington: Christian Lit. Crusade, 1958. Sixteen stimulating sermons on the subject of revival.

————. *The Inextinguishable Blaze*. Grand Rapids: Eerdmans, 1960. A scholarly presentation of spiritual renewal and advance in the eighteenth century.